T0245734

PRAISE FOR *EVERYDAY PR*

"I've read many 'how to' books on PR over my decades-long career. Gina Rubel's *Everyday PR* is a practical, up-to-the-moment primer on what to do and what not to do for novices, students, and PR professionals. Her book provides an overview of public relations and the practical nuts and bolts of its tactical implementation. If you're not hands-on engaged in execution, you might be tempted to gloss over these sections. Read them so you understand the work a PR pro should be doing on your behalf. Among the many things that impressed me about Gina's book is the chapter on Internal Communications. It covers substantive territory that every C-suite executive should be conversant in such as "Building Diversity, Equity, Inclusion, and Belonging into Your Internal Culture and Communications," "Understanding and Eliminating Microaggressions," and "Actionable Steps Companies Can Take to Be Allies to Diverse Communities." I highly recommend this book to anyone who seeks the most current presentation of best practices in communications and business."

— Patrice Tanaka, cofounder of three award-winning PR and marketing agencies, *PRWeek* Hall of Fame inductee, and founder of Joyful Planet

"Gina delivers the advice every executive needs to know. She's down-to-earth, funny, and approachable—everything modern executives need to be when speaking with the press."

—Cesca Antonelli, editor in chief, Bloomberg

"*Everyday PR* provides practical and accessible advice for all types of businesses—non-profit and for-profit alike. It includes real-life examples that lead to achievable results. The book is timely and speaks directly to both long-standing and recent issues I have experienced as the executive director of a statewide advocacy organization. In particular, Gina discusses the importance of ensuring our internal communications practices align with our external ones. Both require significant investment, but the dividends—including high staff morale and organizational effectiveness—will soon follow. Even as someone who has long prioritized sound communication practices, both externally and internally, this book offers valuable lessons on every page. Buy this book."

—Reginald (Reggie) T. Shuford, Esq., executive director, ACLU of Pennsylvania

"Gina Rubel is a master in the field of public relations. Her words of guidance are priceless for absolutely anyone working with the media or interested in public relations."

—Deborah Farone, Farone Advisors LLC

"*Everyday PR: Harnessing Public Relations to Build Relationships, Brands & Businesses* shares valuable insights that help build an online presence via social media, earned media, paid media and more. As a professional storyteller, I can attest that public relations is important because it involves storytelling, and stories have a transformative power to allow us to see the world in a different way than we do if we just encounter it on our own. This book presents unique and helpful ways in which we can catch the attention of our buying audience and engage them. Advertising and marketing can only go so far and can become bothersome at times, turning buyers away. This is one of the best books to guide you through the ups and downs of public relations, raising reputations, and building relationships."

—Susan C. Freeman,
CEO, Freeman Means Business and Conscious Inclusion Company

"Gina Rubel is a superstar in the world of public relations, branding, and marketing. From creating an identifiable and admired reputation to developing a plan to build an image that is aligned with your values and all that you bring to the table, Gina knows how to do it. She provides a helpful, clear and articulate plan that, if followed, can help you to bring your business to the next level."

—Amanda Soler, COO, Central Bucks (Pennsylvania) Chamber of
Commerce, and host of the *SolFul Connections Podcast*

"I'm reviewing this book for an undergraduate course in Writing for Public Relations. I can already see this will be a great resource for media professionals in the field right now. The book delivers up-to-date best practices for writing media releases and pitches while sharing the much-needed perspectives of reporters and content creators. You learn what today's journalists are seeking in a pitch and how to best grab their attention. Whether you are a professional or a student of communication, you'll extract some great tips and fine-tune your skills to reflect today's changing media world."

—Marion Callahan, multimedia journalist
and assistant professor of media, Delaware Valley University

"PR should be part of every brand marketing strategy for every personal brand and business. It is the easiest and most beneficial way to showcase your expertise and provide value to a broader audience. Gina Rubel is a PR and crisis management genius, and you'll find all you need to create a PR strategy in *Everyday PR*. If you are ready to scale your business and stand out in your area of expertise, *Everyday PR* is for you. You'll learn strategies and get valuable insights, tools, and resources from Gina. Her examples are invaluable."

—Robyn Graham, business and mindset mentor,
host of *The Robyn Graham Show*, and author of *You, Me, and Anxiety*

"If you are in the role of business development, then you need to read *Everyday PR* by Gina Rubel. This book simplifies the process of getting PR and suggests easy action steps to increase your visibility. I highly recommend *Everyday PR*!"

—Scott Love, founder/CEO, The Attorney Search Group
and host of *The Rainmaking Podcast*

"PR can be make-or-break for growing companies, and with *Everyday PR*, business leaders will learn from the best what they need to succeed. Gina Rubel is an accomplished practitioner when it comes to legal marketing and law firm public relations, with decades of experience under her belt."

—Naren Aryal, CEO, Amplify Publishing Group

an imprint of Amplify Publishing Group

www.amplifypublishing.com

Everyday PR: Harnessing Public Relations to Build Relationships, Brands & Businesses

For more information, please contact:
Amplify Publishing, an imprint of Amplify Publishing Group
620 Herndon Parkway Suite 320
Herndon, VA 20170
info@amplifypublishing.com

Library of Congress Control Number: 2022908291

CPSIA Code: PRV1222A
ISBN-13: 978-1-63755-510-1

Printed in the United States

To everyone who has ever believed in me—especially my husband, Scott; our children, Gianna and Ford; my mother, Jo-Ann; and my father, Richard (who left this earth too soon)—thank you. You inspire me every day to be my best self.

EVERYDAY
PR

Harnessing Public Relations
to Build Relationships,
Brands & Businesses

GINA F. RUBEL

amplify

TABLE OF CONTENTS

🎤 Throughout the book you will see this icon, which indicates that there is a corresponding podcast to supplement the information shared in the book.

When you see 🎤 "On Record PR Podcast," you can go to www.onrecordpr.com and search for the podcast name or scan the QR code with your mobile device to be directed to the recording.

FOREWORD

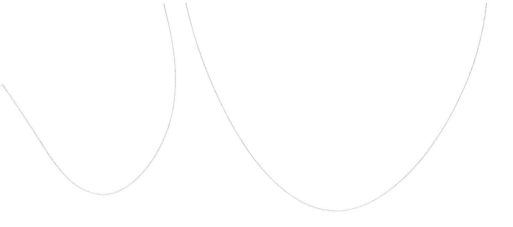

F or more than forty years, I have watched companies grow and prosper because of strategic public relations initiatives.

Before starting Jacobs Consulting & Executive Coaching, which serves agencies and their senior leaders throughout the United States, I spent twenty-five years in management and leadership positions with several public relations agencies, including Ogilvy & Mather PR, Marina Maher Communications, and others. At each of these firms, I served on senior management and leadership committees responsible for staff development, training, morale, recruitment, and retention.

Over those years, I came to know Gina Rubel as a true expert and advisor in PR, reputation and crisis management, and then as a podcaster. And over that time, we became friends.

I was deeply honored when she asked me to read *Everyday PR*, and it's my joy to introduce her to you as the author of this book.

During my career, I have read many business books focused on public relations, marketing, business and leadership development, social media engagement, crisis communications, and all the topics Gina so expertly covers in *Everyday PR*.

Though PR in its early days focused on the acts of publicizing a business and managing a company's reputation, it is important to understand that public relations is much more than that today.

Without publicity and a well-known reputation, a business may have a hard time growing and thriving in its respective industry. A steady stream of efficient integrated communications strategies can help build an audience that equates to stronger retention and acquisition of customers and talent—both of which translate into higher profits.

A common misconception of many small business owners is that PR is only for large companies and recognized brands. As a PR professional for many years, I am here to tell you that PR is for all types of businesses, and *Everyday PR* clearly explains what, when, why, and how.

As I read through *Everyday PR*, I was impressed by a number of things:

1. **ITS PRACTICALITY:** Every strategy, every tactic, and every recommendation is born of common sense and is absolutely doable;

2. **ITS THOROUGHNESS:** I dare you to find a situation, a PR "activation" (oh that word), or communications need that isn't somehow addressed within its pages. More than that, its lists provide every possible implementation and option one might consider within a campaign;

3. **ITS SIMPLICITY:** Simple in its approach. Simple in its language. It's an easy read. In an era when many of us have a number of half-read books throughout our homes, it's nice to have one that you can breeze through in a few hours and feel that you've gained a tremendous amount of knowledge;

4. **HOW CURRENT IT IS FOR OUR TIMES.** Of course, it covers, in great depth, the "basics" like traditional media relations. But it goes beyond this to provide wisdom about a variety of critical issues which today's communicator might face, or for which they'll have to provide counsel, including but not limited to social media, Diversity, Equity, and Inclusion (DE&I), crisis communications, cybersecurity, internal-employee communications, and PR measurement.

Perhaps most important is the fact that Gina's pragmatic, accessible, and forward-thinking framework effectively incorporates public and media relations into an organization's strategic communications plans, thereby increasing the chance it will have a measurable, positive, and sustainable impact on its business.

She walks companies through establishing S.M.A.R.T. business objectives, how to tie those objectives to PR opportunities, how to determine the target audience and key messages, how to persuade that same audience to act as a result of the messages delivered, the public relations rules, tools, strategies, and tactics that help companies to succeed, and how to measure a company's PR investment to ensure it is helping to drive growth and success.

There are many readers for whom this book will bring tremendous value. It speaks to owners of businesses who know they need enhanced relations with their various publics (and doesn't that include every business owner today?). It speaks to those starting out in their PR careers including small agencies and PR soloists who want a more complete understanding of everything they can be doing to bring value to their current clients and prospects.

And attention PR and communications college-level instructors: This book is a must-have resource for you as you plan your coursework if you want to be sure that it brings the newest approaches to PR to your students, who are our industry's future practitioners. Every student of marketing, public relations, and corporate communications should use this guide for strategic and integrated communications.

For all the reasons above, I wholeheartedly encourage you to read and drink in the wisdom of *Everyday PR*. It's a book I know you'll return to again and again as a source of infinite wisdom.

Now turn the page and start reading!

KEN JACOBS
PCC, CPC, ELI-MP

*Readers can hear more from Ken Jacobs on his podcast, On the Air, *which can be found at jacobscomm.com/leadership-executive-coaching-radio and ⚡ On Record PR Podcast: How to Be an Amazingly Effective Leader with Ken Jacobs.*

CHAPTER 1

EVERYDAY PUBLIC RELATIONS: A PRIMER

"IT TAKES TWENTY YEARS TO BUILD A REPUTATION AND FIVE MINUTES TO RUIN IT. IF YOU THINK ABOUT THAT, YOU'LL DO THINGS DIFFERENTLY."

—WARREN BUFFETT

STRATEGIC PUBLIC RELATIONS: THE BASICS

Before you start dreaming about all the television, radio, electronic, and print outlets in which your name and image will appear, take a step back and think strategically about your goals. When was the last time you walked into a business meeting with a prospective client—in person or virtually—without ample preparation?

Much like any successful business, you can only achieve positive publicity and establish a notable reputation through focused, sustained effort. It is important that your expectations be reasonable. In addition, understand that the fruits of your public relations efforts need to grow before they will be ripe for picking, and the growing season depends upon the climate in which they are planted.

DEFINITION OF PUBLIC RELATIONS

Public relations (PR) is different from marketing and advertising and complements both. Public relations is the art and science of proactive advocacy by a company, individual, or brand. It requires strategic management of your position statement and key messages to reach your target audience and, through various tactics, to establish goodwill and mutual understanding.

Effective use of public relations tools allows you to shape public opinion, attitudes, and beliefs. Public relations is much like crafting a pitch for prospective clients or internal stakeholders: you will pains-takingly strategize about what data to present, which heartstrings (if any) you want to tug, the tempo and timing of your delivery, and the information you must deliver to achieve a lasting impact.

ROLE OF PUBLIC RELATIONS

The role of public relations is to help build your organization's brand equity. You communicate key messages to a target audience to elicit a particular response and thus shape public opinion, attitudes, and beliefs.

Public relations allows us to communicate messages about ourselves, our companies, our understanding of the current landscape (political, financial, or social), and the transactions in which we regularly engage.

While public relations, marketing, and advertising differ, all should be considered as part of an organization's integrated marketing mix.

In the big scheme of corporate communications, marketing is the umbrella term under which many forms of communications fall, includ-ing public relations.

Public relations must be a strategic part of a carefully considered integrated marketing plan to complement the company's brand, support its business development and client service efforts, and reinforce other forms of communication.

The most coveted outcome of public relations is earned media, which is unpaid, third-party content that mentions your company, products, services, or individuals typically obtained through media relations.

There also are distinct differences between advertising (also known as paid media) and public relations.

According to marketing software company HubSpot, "Advertising is a [paid] form of communication that attempts to influence the behavior of a defined target audience. Any message developed and placed with the ultimate intention of persuading a group to take a specific action (such as buying a product) can be considered an ad."

I inserted the word "paid" in the definition above because paying to place a message is the primary difference between advertising and public relations, for which media relations is essential.

When you engage with the media, journalists and editors control the messages, as opposed to your organization's marketing team.

Integrated marketing entails the following:

- Account-based marketing
- Advertising
- Awards, ratings, and directories
- Branding
- Business development
- Cause marketing/corporate social responsibility
- Client/customer services
- Community relations
- Content marketing
- Digital marketing
- Direct marketing
- Email marketing
- ESG: environmental, social, and governance
- Events
- Government relations/lobbying
- Influencer marketing
- Media relations
- Partnerships
- Promotions
- Public relations
- Publishing
- Search engine marketing (SEM)
- Search engine optimization (SEO)
- Social media engagement
- Speaker bureaus
- Sponsorships and trade shows
- Video marketing
- Voice marketing
- Websites

The following table details the intrinsic differences between advertising and public relations:

	ADVERTISING	PUBLIC RELATIONS
INSPIRES RECIPIENT OF THE MESSAGE TO:	Respond in some way; call the company or an executive, go to the company's website, fill out a form, send an email	Read more; learn more
IMMEDIATE GOAL IS TO GENERATE:	Leads that result in new business	An understanding or positioning about the company or its services
IMPLICIT GOAL IS:	Profit	Positive perceptions and awareness to support the marketing goal (profit)
MESSAGES, MEDIUMS, TIMING, AND LOCATIONS OF INFORMATION ARE CONTROLLED BY:	The company (paid placements)	Others (such as reporters)
MEASURE OF SUCCESS IS:	The value of new business generated because of the marketing/advertising minus the cost	Expressed in increased awareness, exposure, and trust; share of voice (over the competition); crisis containment, reputation, and message management; differentiation; thought leadership, authority, and influence; and client/customer advocacy

HOW PUBLIC RELATIONS SUPPORTS BUSINESS DEVELOPMENT

Public relations programs are built on effective storytelling, and effective storytelling is what persuades prospective clients or customers to purchase your brand. Public relations is about business development. It's about client and talent retention and acquisition, awareness, education, persuasion, and thought leadership. It's not media stories for media's sake. Any PR person can draft a press release or land a small story. Public relations is about landing the right stories, articles, and thought leadership to support your business goals to grow revenue, increase market share, build awareness, and recruit top talent.

Public relations should position your brand and professionals as leaders in your fields by identifying the unique stories and then crafting pitches and placements that help share those stories with the right audience. Focus on the strategic intersection between business development and public relations through the following:

AWARENESS: One of the prominent roles public relations plays in business development is the generation of knowledge about your business, the industries you serve, your products, your professionals, and/or your locations.

EDUCATION: Once existing and prospective clients and talent have a general awareness about your business or products, public relations is keenly focused on properly educating them about the benefits. Think: What's in it for them?

PERSUASION: Thought leadership opportunities help persuade potential customers to make purchases and prospective employees to apply for job openings.

CREATING A STRONG FOUNDATION FOR YOUR PUBLIC RELATIONS PLAN

Your first step in harnessing the power of public relations is to create a solid foundation on which to build. In this and other ways, creating a public relations plan is like building a new house. It is an exciting time that requires financing, strategic thinking, careful planning, and follow-through. It involves time, attention, and measurable objectives.

When you decide to build a house, you first must determine how much money you will spend. You evaluate your income, expenses, and future needs, as well as allow for the unexpected. Once you know your budget, you determine where you want to live and whether that piece of land will support the house you wish to build. You then engage the right contractors and engineers to test the soil, draw up the plans, get the permits, and so on.

The specifics—like framing materials, exterior parameters, plumbing, and heating—must be determined. You will do all of this and more before you ever decide on the interior details, such as color, trim, lighting, floors, and window treatments. This is no different from creating a strategic and measurable public relations plan for your company. Begin with the plan and objectives before jumping into tactics.

As we explore this topic, keep two things in mind: first, a result—such as being quoted in the press. You cannot get there without first engaging in strategic planning. Second, like a house that you purchase, public relations should be an investment, not an expense.

PUBLIC RELATIONS STRATEGY

Public relations strategy is how you establish your corporate communications efforts' long-term objectives to reach your target audience and elicit a positive reaction.

Strategy also includes how you allocate the resources needed to implement your plan. Determine a manageable timeline and designate the benchmarks against which you will measure your efforts' success.

You will rely on this strategy to reach your target audience and convey your messages, as well as to form the foundation of your public relations plan.

You certainly would not begin to build the walls of your house without first identifying your budget, where the house should be located, the style of home you want to build, the number and size of the rooms you need, and the foundation necessary to build a home that will remain standing.

THE TACTICS

The tools we use to deliver effective public relations strategies are called tactics. PR tactics are like the special amenities we use to enhance our homes. We might install crown molding, granite countertops, and custom cabinets to add beauty and value to our homes. Similarly, we can use publicity, community relations, special events, speaking engagements, sponsorships, and other forms of proactive tactics to mold public opinion.

It should be noted, however, that reactive, ad hoc public relations tactics—sending out a press release, staging an open house, sponsoring an industry event, hosting a press conference—are rarely effective and sometimes dangerous without having first determined your strategy. It's like purchasing furniture for your home before you have a floor plan.

Just as we can't expect a house to be built in one day, public relations activities will not increase business overnight. Harnessing the impact and power of public relations is a long-term, strategic commitment that incorporates many approaches to achieve an organization's goals. Thus, you build a sustainable house.

Your strategy is the blueprint of your public relations home. The tactics are the amenities, furniture, and decorations that allow you to enjoy the benefits.

Public relations, when done right, allows you to build a portfolio of articles, news clippings, videos, and thought leadership content that helps to establish credibility objectively. If correctly employed and implemented, public relations will raise awareness about your services or products and position you as a go-to expert in your field.

Public relations is beneficial in nearly every industry to allow businesses to promote their products and services and their importance to the marketplace and the community at large.

A solid public relations program should build favorable awareness of your organization and its products or services, position you as knowledgeable within your industry and geography, position you as a valuable contributor to the marketplace, create an environment that enhances goodwill among your target audience, educate and persuade your target audience, and provide measurable value to you and your company.

Now, let's determine the specifications for your new public relations plan.

EIGHT STEPS FOR DEVELOPING A STRATEGIC PUBLIC RELATIONS PLAN

To develop and execute a strategic public relations plan, you must employ an eight-step process. These steps are essential.

1. Establish your goals and objectives.

2. Define how you want to be perceived.

3. Determine your target audience.

4. Establish your key message—what you want and need to say.

5. Decide what you want your target audience to do (call to action).

6. Identify which tactics will persuade your target audience to act how you want them to.

7. Implement each tactic to generate optimal results.

8. Measure successes against your goals and objectives.

This eight-step process is explained in detail in chapter 2.

Returning to the home-building analogy, first determine where you want to live (strategy). Then decide what type of house you want to live in (perception/position).

Next, define who will live in the house (target audience). Then explain to the architect how you want to live and how you plan to use your living space (key message).

The architect will design your home and grounds so you can use them the way you would like (call to action).

The builder will construct the house so you can enjoy the space in the intended manner (tactics). Once the house is complete, it will be furnished and decorated with the amenities that allow you to live in style and comfort (implementation).

Finally, when all is said and done, walk across the street, look up at the house, and say, "Wow, what a great investment we've made. It has already appreciated in value and was a sound use of our resources" (measurement).

A director of marketing at a professional service firm in Chicago said she seeks to support business development efforts with public relations initiatives by encouraging the professionals to "speak publicly, draft articles, and participate on panels. It is all great content to repurpose on social media and in online biographies."

She noted that clients and potential clients already know that background information about professionals. The information is generally available on their website biographies and on their LinkedIn profiles. By demonstrating sound thought leadership and presenting their know-how—the way they think and how well they understand the issues and needs of their clients—there is greater validation, which produces better results.

What all this means is that your public relations plan must seamlessly integrate with your organization's overall business and marketing plans. The public relations plan allows you to state your goals and detail how you will achieve them by adopting a proactive mindset. You must look for ways to get out in front of a story or opportunity. Create your own news and events. Set the agenda. Frame the issues, and garner positive publicity for your organization.

Business executives have countless encounters with target audiences and have control over their messaging in person, online, on social media, and over the phone. Create messages that will leave a positive, lasting impression.

What it comes down to is accepting that there are myriad public relations opportunities for professionals to communicate directly with clients and customers, prospective clients and customers, referral sources, and others every day.

Each interaction should be meaningful.

CHAPTER 2

STEPS IN CORPORATE PUBLIC RELATIONS PLANNING

"PUBLICITY IS ABSOLUTELY CRITICAL. A GOOD PR STORY IS
INFINITELY MORE EFFECTIVE THAN A FRONT-PAGE AD."

—RICHARD BRANSON

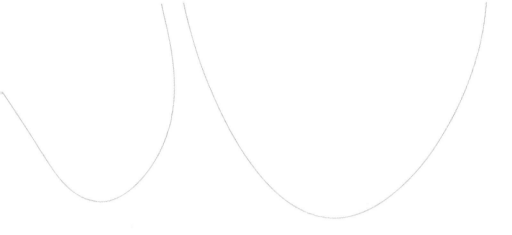

G reat public relations can accelerate business development cycles, increase audience awareness, and help promote rapid growth. Harnessing this power can be a terrific boost—if you proceed with clear objectives and remain true to your core business goals.

To organize your objectives, I have included a tearaway sheet in the appendix on which you can write down ideas.

STEP 1: ESTABLISH YOUR BUSINESS OBJECTIVES

ASK: WHAT ARE MY CORE BUSINESS GOALS? (QUANTIFIABLE)

Understand your business goals or key performance indicators (KPIs). This is the first step in defining measurable objectives for a corporate public relations program. When you measure your public relations program's value, you substantiate that PR has furthered your overall plan.

A company's business goals must be S.M.A.R.T. Without something to measure, the strategic plans get sucked into a black hole. S.M.A.R.T. goal setting is not a new concept, and it is certainly not a concept that I invented. It is a strategic formula for setting yourself up for success.

Goals must be S.M.A.R.T.:
- Specific: illustrative with real numbers, actual results
- Measurable: quantifiable, which means you must first set a baseline
- Achievable: realistic goals are those that will most likely succeed
- Relevant: it must make sense under the circumstances
- Timely: both in terms of relevance and being completed within a set amount of time

Examples of quantifiable goals (or KPIs):
- Increase profitability by 15 percent
- Increase sales by 20 percent
- Expand into new markets through organic growth or mergers and acquisitions
- Develop new products or services
- Focus on a niche business area to shed unprofitable corporate segments
- Increase the number of employees by 10 percent
- Increase the organization's net promoter score (NPS)
- Grow the company's geographic footprint by 20 percent

Quantifiable goals incorporate something that is measurable.

Now that you have identified your business goals, determine your public relations objectives, which must be S.M.A.R.T.

What do you hope to accomplish by executing a public relations plan?

What do you want people to think, say, or do when they hear your name?

Executives should ask these questions when embarking on a public relations initiative. The answers will help draft the blueprint of your plan and determine the best tools for implementation.

To get started ask how public relations can help achieve your quantifiable business goals and what public relations can do more effectively than other disciplines. Once you have answered these questions, you can define your public relations objectives.

Typical public relations objectives (general and specific):

- Increase awareness about your company and its products or services
- Build name recognition of your organization, its executives, and its products or services
- Announce a merger, acquisition, or office relocation to facilitate easy communication between your company and its clients or customers
- Increase new business and profits
- Retain or grow existing client accounts
- Acquire prospective clients in a new market segment
- Create demand and interest from prospective employees
- Develop employee goodwill
- Garner media attention regarding a successful business venture, product development, charitable initiative, or expansion
- Generate referrals from thought leaders
- Manage your company's (or your personal) reputation

With the digital age of communication, you can use public relations to create a two-way conversation with your target audience.

STEP 2: DEFINE HOW YOU WANT YOUR COMPANY AND ITS EXECUTIVES TO BE PERCEIVED

ASK: HOW DO YOU WANT PEOPLE TO PERCEIVE YOU OR YOUR BUSINESS?

What do you want people to think, say, or do when they hear about you, your company, or your services or products? How do you want to be positioned or perceived? What type of business lifestyle do you lead? This is your position statement.

Below are examples of some popular brands' and organizations' position statements, all of which were found on their websites:

- Target exists "to help all families discover the joy of everyday life. That's *our purpose*. Our mission. The promise of surprises, fun, ease and inspiration at every turn, no matter when, where or how you shop."
- "Founded in 2004, Facebook's mission is to give people the power to build community and bring the world closer together. People use Facebook to stay connected with friends and family, to discover what's going on in the world, and to share and express what matters to them."
- "PBS is a membership organization that, in partnership with its member stations, serves the American public with programming and services of the highest quality, using media to educate, inspire, entertain, and express a diversity of perspectives."
- Amazon's "mission is to be Earth's most customer-centric company. Amazon is guided by four principles: customer obsession rather than competitor focus, passion for invention, commitment to operational excellence, and long-term thinking."
- "The mission of Harvard College is to educate the citizens and citizen-leaders for our society. We do this through our commitment to the transformative power of a liberal arts and sciences education."

I work with companies of all sizes, yet there are clear differences in how each one positions itself. Know how you are differentiating your organization and its offerings. How is your company positioned?

The way to answer this question from the perception of others is to determine how your organization is perceived.

Ask your significant other to tell you what you do. Jot down the response. Do the same thing with your best friend, closest neighbor, parents, employees, children, colleagues in other industries, and business associates. If everyone answers, "Well, you're an executive [or insert title here] at XYZ Company," then you're barely there. My response is, "So what? It doesn't matter that you're a corporate executive." The question is: What purpose does your business prowess serve?

If you are the owner of a local family-owned grocery store or a high-powered corporate executive who makes millions and generates multimillion-dollar deals, you may wish to be perceived as such.

You want the most important audience to perceive you the way you want and need to be perceived.

If you can walk the walk, you can talk the talk for purchasers and potential purchasers of your services or products.

Once you have decided how you want to be perceived, there are two things to be communicated in your position statement: the features of your organization and how they benefit your target audience.

FEATURES VS. BENEFITS

Although entire seminars and books are devoted to explaining the differences between features and benefits, here is the answer briefly: Features are the characteristics that physically describe your products, services, background, or experiences. Benefits are why your products or services matter to the recipient.

A crystal wineglass is crystal. It is clear. It is solid. These are its features, not its benefits. Most professionals' biographies and LinkedIn profiles communicate features about the individuals—not the benefits of working with them. They include the individual's areas of expertise, their education and professional background, and all the other "about" information that is typical in a professional biography.

The benefits of the crystal wineglass are that you can see through the container to identify the liquid inside, the object is weighted so it can't easily tip over, the object is pure and doesn't give off any flavor changers or odors that would distort the flavor, and the shape complements the bouquet of the wine for maximum enjoyment.

The benefits of working with a business executive should describe how the individual's experience best positions them to provide a product or service.

Features establish credibility and distinguish your background from that of your competitors. Benefits tell your audience what they will gain by working with you or your organization. In other words, the benefits explain why your products or services matter to the end user.

In highly regulated industries, such as finance and law, benefits language is highly scrutinized because you cannot present information that is subjective.

Now that you know how you want to be perceived, ask whether your aspirations are reasonable.

A lawyer from a small town with a population of fewer than nine thousand people once told me that he wanted to be known as "the best" lawyer in his state, which had a population of 12.3 million and nearly 100,000 licensed lawyers. He believed that he should be on CNN, MSNBC, *The Today Show*, and *Good Morning America*. This lawyer had retired from the practice of law several years before and wanted to make "a comeback." Moreover, he had not conveyed any information that was unique, earth-shattering, or important to a mass audience. His aspirations were not realistic for his circumstances.

Conversely, a former prosecutor in the Bill Cosby case reached out to me to seek representation before Cosby's sentencing hearing. Bill Cosby, often referred to as "America's Dad" in pop culture, was convicted of three counts of aggravated indecent assault. It shocked the nation, and the conviction had a massive effect on the Philadelphia region where Cosby was revered as a hometown hero.

Our client, Stewart Ryan, was a crucial part of the prosecution team in the conviction of Bill Cosby on charges of sexual assault. Stewart was the only assistant district attorney to remain with the Montgomery County prosecutor's office from the time of Cosby's arrest through his conviction. Stewart successfully prosecuted this historic case and was later commended by Montgomery County District Attorney Kevin Steele for "his legal acumen, courtroom skills, commitment to seeking justice for all sexual assault victims, and outstanding leadership."

Stewart had previously been barred from speaking to the media when he worked for the district attorney but could speak publicly after the sentencing hearing. His aim was to position himself as a thought leader on sexual assault cases to support his civil law practice. My company, Furia Rubel Communications, Inc., achieved this goal through extensive research, targeted media pitching, and monitoring of the reporters who were covering the story and what they needed from their sources during the peak of the news cycle.

Because Stewart had a story to tell and the expertise to back it up, and because the timing was right, we were able to secure significant media placements. Following the sentencing hearing, Stewart was interviewed by the Associated Press, the *New York Times*, *The Legal Intelligencer*, and the ABC and NBC affiliates in Philadelphia.

We also arranged an appearance on *Good Morning America* the following day where Stewart appeared on a panel with Gloria Allred, a feminist lawyer who represents dozens of Cosby's other victims, and Lise-Lotte Lublin, a Cosby survivor, to discuss the sentencing with the show's anchor, George Stephanopoulos.

Thereafter, Stewart was invited to the *Philadelphia Inquirer*'s newsroom to watch Dr. Christine Blasey Ford and Judge Brett Kavanaugh's testimony regarding sexual assault allegations with other local experts, including Carol Tracy, executive director of the Women's Law Project; Robin Fierstein, licensed psychologist who specializes in trauma; and Mary Onama, executive director of the Victim Services Center in Montgomery County, Pennsylvania. The commentary that followed positioned Stewart as a thought leader for topics related to sexual assault and victim advocacy.

There is a stark difference between the retired lawyer who wanted to be on *Good Morning America* and Stewart Ryan, who had something of value to add to the discussion.

Setting reasonable goals and objectives is half the battle in successful public relations planning.

STEP 3: IDENTIFY YOUR TARGET AUDIENCE

ASK: WHOM DO YOU WANT TO INFLUENCE?

Determine exactly who you want to influence. This is your target audience. It should be defined as precisely and as accurately as possible. Your target audience should be the thought leaders and decision makers who will ultimately affect your company's bottom line.

For most organizations, the target audience includes current and past clients or customers, prospective clients or customers, industry referral sources, and employees.

What about the thought leaders who influence their decisions? They can be union leaders, corporate executives, chambers of commerce, trade association and community leaders, clergy, government officials, family members and friends, activists, and the media, among others.

After you define each target audience, dig a little deeper. This is the most challenging task for large corporations because they usually consist of many divisions, all with a different audience. Break down each division, product, or service and its corresponding target audience.

To hit the mark with your public relations program, determine where your target audience is located. Are they local, regional, national, or global? Identify the industries in which your target audience works and, if they are corporate clients, the titles of the decision makers. Research the publications and programs they read, listen to, and view and the blogs, podcasts, or other forms of electronic and social media to which they subscribe. Determine the conferences, seminars, or town meetings they attend; the size of the businesses by revenue or number of employees for which they work, their age and income bracket; and who influences their buying decisions.

When you've answered these questions, ask one more question: What are my target audience's needs, and how can I meet them?

STEP 4: ESTABLISH YOUR KEY MESSAGES

ASK: WHAT DO YOU WANT AND NEED TO SAY?

Once you have defined how you want to be perceived and who you are trying to reach, determine what you want and need to say. This is referred to as your "key messages."

Your key messages are thoughts, words, or phrases that embody the fundamental ideas that you and your organization would like to express to your target audience. They must be clear, concise, and memorable. Your key messages must align with your business objectives. These are the thoughts you want your audience to remember above all else. They ensure consistency so you and other members of your company speak with one voice to your target audience.

Your primary key messages are the sine qua non for the foundation of your public relations and marketing plans. Focusing on a few key messages is vital to effective communication: who you are, what you do (features), what your clients or customers need from you, and what services or products and benefits you will deliver to them.

Create secondary key messages that communicate the nature of underlying or derivative needs. Secondary key messages are used to communicate specific needs or wants that may arise during your business practices. They reinforce your primary key messages and then focus on a particular issue, fact, or need. In addition, your secondary key messages should vary depending on what you're trying to accomplish.

For example, you might want retail consumers to be aware that your organization spearheaded an initiative to donate products to underserved populations. Your business is still conveying the primary key message that you produce a specific product; however, your secondary key message will be tailored to influence the buyers and build goodwill (charitable initiative) rather than focus on the overall nature of your company.

Once you have determined the key messages that reinforce your goals and objectives and have tailored them to the needs and wants of your target audience, determine what you want your audience to do in response to your messages.

STEP 5: CRAFT YOUR CALL TO ACTION

ASK: WHAT DO YOU WANT YOUR TARGET AUDIENCE TO THINK, SAY, OR DO BECAUSE OF YOUR MESSAGE?

Ask what you want your target audience to think, say, or do when they hear your message. Do you want them to purchase your product, or do you want them to refer a certain type of business to your company? Would you like them to be aware that you exist in case they need your services or products in the future?

Understand what you want to happen because of communicating your key messages, which should support your company's business objectives and thus be quantifiable.

According to Leslie Richards, chief innovation officer of Furia Rubel Communications, Inc., and a digital marketing expert for more than two decades, "Crafting the right call to action requires careful consideration of where your audience is in the decision-making process and how much exposure they may have had to your brand or your offer. For example, if your audience is getting to know you or your offer, a call to action that reads 'register now' or 'book an appointment' is premature. They will likely need more information before they can feel comfortable to act. A more effective call to action might read 'learn more' or 'meet the team.'"

The call to action can also be tested. This is something known in the marketing industry as "A/B testing." This is when you take two or more versions of your call to action and use them with different communications to see which one your audience is more receptive to. It is a way to gather data that helps you identify which call to action will be the most effective.

Next, determine how you will convince your target audience to respond to your message. Which tactics will reach them to accomplish your public relations objectives?

STEP 6: PERSUADE YOUR TARGET AUDIENCE TO ACT

ASK: WHAT DOES MY TARGET AUDIENCE WANT AND NEED?

You can employ various public relations tactics to create an ongoing buzz. Tactics designed to increase awareness among your target clients or customers, generate recognition, and position you or your product as an industry leader will increase your bottom line. By consistently and productively executing strategic public relations tactics, you can build momentum and increase your bottom line.

The best way to determine which tactics will work is to identify the typical activities, desires, and needs of your audience. For example, if your business is built predominantly on referrals, consider presenting a seminar to an audience of potential referral sources. If your business is built on credibility in a particular industry sector, consider getting involved as a thought leader in a professional association, writing for the association's publication, blogging on thought leadership topics relevant to the industry, and being a go-to resource.

After you identify your target audience, it is time to determine what they want and need. You do not have to invest significant amounts of money to make this determination. You can do the research by asking your ideal clients or customers to respond. Call upon thought leaders in your sphere of influence to explore what makes them tick.

Conduct secondary research to uncover general data that will help you make the best decisions. For example, what types of questions does your target audience ask on social media? What are the issues that keep them up at night?

Search Twitter to identify what your audience is talking about. Join Facebook or LinkedIn groups relevant to your products or services. Search the internet for frequently asked questions that relate to your offerings. Ask people among your target audience what they want and need and how they make purchasing decisions.

The persuasive strategy should determine and articulate the pains you can alleviate and the problems you can solve on behalf of your clients or customers.

You also can conduct client/customer surveys to verify their wishes and needs. Proceed with caution, however, because surveys may divulge information or critiques about your organization that you are not willing or able to address or respond to. In that event, you will find yourself in a less favorable situation.

Compile a list of sources and industry events that your target audience uses to stay up to date. Do they religiously attend industry conferences? Do they have a savvy public relations program for which they publicize an award, or are they networking regularly within an industry association? This will be beneficial for you to reach your target audience without deviating.

If you want to generate publicity that will reach your target audience, identify the publications they typically read and to which they subscribe. Once you know the media outlets trusted by your audience, you can target your media outreach accordingly.

Identify the decision makers who select the sector of products or services in which you operate. Observe their selection process criteria. Recognize and understand the trends in your target audiences' lives and businesses and decide which types of programs (tactics) you can develop to respond to those trends.

As a business owner who may be limited to personal networking, get involved with your local or state trade organizations, participate in your undergraduate or graduate school alumni associations, join a chamber of commerce committee, or actively participate in your religious institution. Professional networking also includes maximizing the value of social media tools, which you can do at any time from any location.

As your network expands, look to your organization's culture and expectations to define ways to enhance your name and stature in the community.

If you work in a company that has a marketing department, now is the time for you to meet with the chief marketing officer (CMO), chief business development officer (CBDO), public relations director, or marketing director. Ask what you can do to assist with public relations.

In larger organizations, it is not typically an executive's job to issue press releases or organize continuing education programs to reach your target audience. Your company will have procedures in place (and if not, it is time to establish them) for marketing and public relations. The CMO, CBDO, and other marketing professionals will be thrilled if you avail yourself.

In the larger companies, it is also likely that the organization will dictate the type of public relations you may pursue, but you can find opportunities by analyzing who you are and where your interests lie. Identify your passions and how you can parlay them into promotional opportunities, then determine which are most appealing.

Most of the time, you will want to employ multiple tactics so you are not a blip on your audience's screen. You want more than fifteen minutes of fame.

STEP 7: IMPLEMENT TACTICS TO GENERATE RESULTS

ASK: WHAT WILL CAUSE PEOPLE TO ACT (TACTICS)?

Implementation is the how-to in corporate public relations. It is the actual performance of tactics to reach your target audience with your key messages to effectuate your goals and objectives. This is the subject of most of this book.

There are many tactics that may draw the attention of your target audience, including articles (published) and advertorials, awards, rankings and recognitions, book publishing, content marketing, commentary, special events and initiatives, letters to the editor, opinion editorials (op-eds), press conferences, social media engagement, speaking engagements, survey and trend results, thought leadership, and white papers.

If you're a corporate executive, you may have a limited amount of time to devote to public relations. In this case, capitalize on one or two simple tactics like writing articles or blog posts and having them published in trade or consumer outlets.

Follow the rule of COPES: create once, publish enthusiastically and strategically.

This acronym used to be known as "create once, publish everywhere"; however, "everywhere" is misleading. If you publish an article or blog, send it to relevant customers and prospects; share it on social media sites like LinkedIn, Twitter, and Facebook; and include it in the company's e-newsletter. Check out chapter 10 for more details.

STEP 8: MEASURE PUBLIC RELATIONS OUTCOMES

ASK: HOW CAN I MEASURE MY PUBLIC RELATIONS EFFORTS?

With the pressure to be competitive and to acquire and retain more talent and clients, businesses must implement their marketing and public relations plans thoroughly. Few take the time to measure the effectiveness of their communications.

How will your company know for certain that 80 percent of new business came from referrals or that the community event you hosted did or did not generate new clients?

Since the topic of public relations measurement (covered in chapter 12) can be the subject of a white paper, what follows is a list of measurement tools to have in your arsenal. When combined, they are called your TechStack.

Public relations and marketing measurement tools:

- Agility PR
- Bandwidth
- Burrelles
- CARMA International
- Cision | TrendKite
- Converseon
- CoverageBook
- Critical Mention
- Digimind
- Falcon AI
- Google Analytics
- HubSpot
- Meltwater
- Memo
- Mention
- Muck Rack
- Nielsen
- Onclusive
- PublicRelay
- RepTrak
- Signal AI
- Sprinklr
- Sprout Social
- Talkwalker
- Trust Insights
- UNICEPTA

If you do not measure your public relations, you are only partially communicating. You created a solid public relations plan, targeted your audience, identified your positions, crafted your messages, laid out your calls to action, and implemented tactics. But you are only three-quarters of the way there. To complete the process, you must measure the results. Without measuring results, you are wasting the money you spent on creating and implementing your plan. Make the investment to build your strategic, sustainable, and influential public relations plan.

CHAPTER 3

PUTTING THE MEDIA TO WORK FOR YOU

"IT IS ALWAYS A RISK TO SPEAK TO THE PRESS: THEY ARE LIKELY TO REPORT WHAT YOU SAY."

—HUBERT H. HUMPHREY

When the opportunity to work with the media arises, be well prepared and media trained to ensure that everything will run smoothly and effectively.

Companies and their representatives can and should control, to the extent possible, all messages provided to the media.

Media relations can be a productive way to enhance an individual's or organization's reputation and to represent stakeholders' best interests.

If you are interested in increasing your media exposure, this is most easily accomplished by developing personal relationships with reporters who cover your industry.

CORPORATE MEDIA POLICY PRIMER

All companies, no matter how big or small, should have a written media policy.

The owner of a five-person professional service business once contacted me for advice after the co-owner was indicted and arrested for illegal sexual conduct. The news of the arrest was covered in every major media outlet in the city where the arrest took place—the same city where the company was located. Reporters immediately began calling the office, and the receptionist responded by saying, "No comment." The receptionist had no authority to speak with the media, but the company had no media policy and never instructed the staff how to deal with media calls. The media thus reported that the company had "no comment," which did not position them in a favorable light.

Media training is imperative for everyone at the organization, not just those authorized to speak with the media. The onus is on the company to position all employees for success in the event a journalist contacts them. As a rule, empower employees to request information rather than give it. For instance, the receptionist in the previous example should have requested as much information as possible (the reporter's name, contact information, media outlet, and deadline) rather than shutting down the conversation with an unfavorable "no comment."

Your company's media policy should provide a list of who may speak with the media on the company's behalf (spokespersons). It also must include detailed protocols for handling media queries for an interview or statement, including record keeping procedures for media calls, emails, and interviews; details of what the spokesperson or representative may and may not say; guidance on how to handle queries about clients/customers and issues in which the organization is not involved but has industry or subject-matter expertise; direction on how the company will handle media when it deals with a legal matter; an outline of the organization's crisis communications, disaster recovery, and incident response procedures; guidance on how to handle any issues particular to your industry, including any ethics issues related to dealing with the media; and advice for complying with any legal requirements with respect to communicating in highly regulated industries, such as law, finance, and health care, if applicable.

FIVE TIPS TO MAXIMIZE RELATIONSHIPS WITH THE MEDIA

To maximize the value of your media relationships:

1. **DETERMINE YOUR PRIMARY GEOGRAPHIC MARKET:** This could be a particular city, a geographic region, or a national or an international audience.

2. **CREATE A PREFERRED MEDIA LIST (PML):** Compile a list of newspapers, television and radio stations, newsletters, alumni publications, magazines, blogs, and podcasts that reach your target audience. Several publications and databases such as Cision, Muck Rack, and others include listings of media contacts.

3. **DOUBLE-CHECK YOUR CONTACT FILE:** Verify your list of contact names, email addresses, and phone numbers. Ensure they cover your topic or industry. If you are not sure, check their LinkedIn and Twitter profiles.

4. **KNOW WHO YOU ARE PITCHING:** Become familiar with the media outlets on your list. Read the publications and blogs, watch the television programs, listen to the radio shows and podcasts, and get to know their individual content and style, especially that of the reporters you plan to pitch. Reporters often are assigned a beat (subject matter) to cover. Take the time to acquaint yourself with who they are and what they cover.

5. **UPDATE YOUR PML REGULARLY:** Update your list at least quarterly and any time you make media calls or find out that someone new is covering your beat. Job changes are common in journalism, especially considering the continuing decline in print advertising sales, which has led to frequent restructuring and consolidation of media outlets and their publishers/owners.

Once you have assembled and verified your media list, get to know the journalists you are pitching. Send news about your business, story ideas, and trends only to the media outlets that cover your issues.

CRAFT AN EFFECTIVE AND CONCISE INTRODUCTION

Also known as an elevator speech, a concise introduction is a clear, brief statement about who you are and how you can benefit your target audience. This statement should support how you want people to perceive you: your reputation.

People move faster and have shorter attention spans than ever. Articulate who you are and what you do quickly and effectively before you lose the attention of your audience.

Have a compelling and creative statement ready. Use it when you meet people for the first time and they ask about your business, as your outgoing voicemail message, in your prospective client meetings, at the conference table, when pitching the media, and anywhere you discuss your business.

Many professionals find it challenging to produce a solid introduction, an effective statement that is prepared, rehearsed, and ready when networking, contacting the media, or talking to a prospective customer or employer.

Start with a brief and memorable introduction. State who you are, what you do, and how your work benefits others. Make it easy to understand and compelling enough to leave the listener wanting to know more. If done well, your introduction should invite more detailed and qualifying questions.

For example:

I'm Gina Rubel, the founder and CEO of Furia Rubel Communications. I collaborate with corporate and law firm leaders for high-stakes public relations, crisis planning, and incident response support, including high-profile litigation media relations.

Do:
- Understand that every word matters.
- Be specific.
- Engage your listeners, grab their attention, and get them interested in the conversation.

- Be familiar with the benefits to your listeners (what is in it for them).
- Concentrate on what the listener wants and needs to hear.
- Keep in mind your tone of voice.
- Be enthusiastic.
- Invest time to revise your personal statement as you gain experience.
- Keep your introduction current.
- Keep your introduction short.

Do not:
- Summarize your job description and call that your introduction.
- Use general language or jargon.
- Sound like a salesperson.
- Speak in a monotone voice.
- Memorize your introduction word for word.
- Cross your arms and look down at the floor while speaking.
- Compare yourself or your company to your competition.
- Appear rehearsed.

When you meet someone for the first time, you have only a few seconds to make a memorable impression—make the most of it.

Use the tool in the appendix to help craft your introduction.

EFFECTIVE WAYS TO GARNER CORPORATE MEDIA COVERAGE

Good press is a vital component of corporate communications, and you must understand how to best relate to reporters.

Pitching a reporter or producer can be akin to throwing a ball to the batter to see whether they are going to hit it and, if so, how far. Even though the commonly known terminology is "pitching," it is the art of communicating and having a conversation.

"I think there's a lot more sophistication now around how companies are pitching those of us in the media, when they're pitching us, and what they're pitching to us," said Robert Ambrogi of LawSites.

 On Record PR Podcast: What LegalTech Journalists Want to Know, with Bob Ambrogi of LawSites

There is no single way to pitch a story. Understanding the nuances of the media, however, will help you become a better media resource overall.

DO YOUR HOMEWORK: Research the reporter before contacting them. Know the reporter's beat (what types of articles this person writes and from where they obtain information). Be familiar with articles that the reporter has written in the past, and if you can, tie one of them in with your pitch.

"I get pitches that use the wrong name or the wrong media outlet," said Kelly Phillips Erb, journalist at Bloomberg Tax.

"But the thing that I would say is I love it when people do their homework. It's frustrating to me when people do not. I get a lot of pitches, and we joke about this on Twitter a lot, like during tax season when people will say things like, 'Dear Kelly, you might not know, but it's the middle of tax season.' I then say to myself, 'Why would you start that way?' Because first, I'm a tax attorney. Secondly, I write about tax news, and thirdly, it's March. Even people who don't do those things for a living know it's tax season."

She said, "I love pitches when people do their homework. I dislike pitches that feel generic. I dislike pitches that suggest to me that you've sent it to ten different organizations without regard for what they do."

 On Record PR Podcast: Bloomberg Tax Journalist Kelly Phillips Erb, aka @Taxgirl, Talks Media Relations, Diversity, and How Taxes Are Fun

UNDERSTAND DEADLINES: The worst time to contact a reporter is when they are on deadline. Ascertain whether it is a suitable time before discussing your story. If the reporter says it is a bad time, ask when a better time would be to call back and then do so at the specified time. If yours is a breaking news story, let the reporter know. The reporter will decide whether they wish to learn more at that time. If it is that important and the reporter is interested, they will likely ask for more information.

BE MEMORABLE: Reporters receive hundreds of emails, calls, and social media pitches daily. Your story must stand out. Be specific and brief—this will show the reporter that you are not wasting their time. Differentiate your story from others and leave a compelling impression to stand out.

LEVERAGE VARIOUS FORMS OF MEDIA: There are many forms of media to leverage, including online, print, radio, television, podcasts, and more.

Marion Callahan, multimedia journalist, said, "Multimedia reporting is about telling stories in every way possible. The idea of multitasking is no longer something extra that a journalist does. It's part of what everyone does as a modern storyteller. We don't only go into a room with a notepad and a pen. I'm looking at grabbing information through audio and video, telling stories through photographs and slideshows. I look at the situation and think, 'Am I going to create one video, or do I have to create a one-minute video for Twitter?'

"Not only do we think about how we're gathering the news, but we think about how we are going to get to our readers because our audience is different. Most of our readers are no longer waiting for the paper in the morning. They want to read news twenty-four hours a day. We must find a way to reach them and think creatively to do it and in many different storytelling forms."

☆ On Record PR Podcast: Reporting the News as a Multimedia Journalist with Marion Callahan

SAY YES: Amanda M. Soler, chief operating officer of the Central Bucks County Chamber of Commerce in Pennsylvania, said, "Say yes! When a reporter asks you to share business tips or expertise, be responsive. Don't wait. Saying yes propels you to your next level. When you succeed, congratulations—you just moved up a step."

Soler also advises people to author articles for their Chamber of Commerce's newsletter, blog, and/or magazine. She said, "If you aren't comfortable writing, compile a top ten tips lists. Share information pertinent to your trade and do so utilizing the chamber's publications. It is one of the many benefits of membership."

AMPLIFY YOUR MESSAGE ON SOCIAL MEDIA: "LinkedIn has become a publishing platform, one of the largest [business-to-business] publishers in the world," said Devin Banerjee, a senior member of the editorial team at LinkedIn. "We're seeing that trend continue and even accelerate. We've seen public content on LinkedIn grow about 29 percent year over year during the past year. It is important to think about your audiences on LinkedIn."

☆ On Record PR Podcast: Leveraging LinkedIn to Develop Business, Attract Top Talent, and Become a Thought Leader with Devin Banerjee

"I'm a millennial, so social media has always been there for me," said Lizzy McLellan, former business of law editor at ALM Global, LLC. "I do think it says something when we're learning about someone, or we're hoping to interview them for a story, or maybe we're writing about their lateral. I'll look at their LinkedIn page and try to get an idea of what they've done before. I want to see other law firms or businesses they've worked for and see what some of their accomplishments are. That's not to take the place of asking questions and having a great conversation with them, but it's helpful."

 🎙 *On Record PR Podcast: How ALM's Global Newsroom Is Covering the Business of Law in a Coronavirus World with Lizzy McLellan*

Similarly, Sara Merken, legal reporter at Reuters, said, "I'm on Twitter a lot. It's usually in the background of what I'm doing because a lot of times I'll see something on Twitter before a press release or before someone reaches out. Not as much for court filings. Those I'm usually more proactive about finding, but Twitter is a big one for finding news or just knowing what people are saying about the news that I also might be writing about. People are talking about 'why this matters' or 'what this means' in the broader context."

 🎙 *On Record PR Podcast: Trends in Legal Media with Reuters's Legal Reporter Sara Merken*

KNOW MEDIA FREQUENCY: Reporters working for a daily publication or newscast will be interested in a news story that they can break to the public. Conversely, reporters working for weekly publications or feature programs are more interested in detailed, comprehensive information and how that information will affect the business community. Modify your story and strategy accordingly to avoid getting filtered out. These are not steadfast rules. Oftentimes weeklies will break news online any day of the week and may go into greater detail in the print edition.

DO NOT SELL ANYTHING: When you are providing the media with news or a resource for information, you are not selling your services. Do not send brochures, newsletters, or other marketing materials. Engage them in a meaningful conversation that will help them report your story or make you a go-to resource to be quoted in other stories.

Joan Feldman, cofounder and editor in chief at Attorney at Work, said she receives pitches with "subject lines that say, 'I need to be on your site,' or 'I will pay you twenty-five dollars for a link.' The competition for an editor's attention is intense, and it's not only PR agencies or in-house marketers, but it's also SEO agencies, content marketing agencies, and a lot of 'spammy' players who are looking to get backlinks on credible websites. Be yourself, be authentic, do your homework. And it's OK to follow up many times if you're offering credible information. If you're a spammer, leave me alone."

 On Record PR Podcast: The Dos and Don'ts of Pitching Articles to Attorney at Work with Joan Feldman, Cofounder and Editor in Chief

GO THE EXTRA MILE—HELP REPORTERS SEE BOTH SIDES OF THE STORY: Reporters must not mislead their readers. Think like a journalist. Help create a balanced story by taking the extra step and providing reporters with opposing perspectives. Showing both sides of a story makes it hard for the reporter to accuse you of being disingenuous or biased.

USING VOICEMAIL TO PITCH EFFECTIVELY

What does your voicemail recording say about you?

When was the last time you listened to your outgoing office or cell phone voicemail messages?

While email, texting, and social media are the prevalent forms of communication, a voicemail is still often the first time someone interacts with you. Before recording your voicemail message, write down what you plan to say.

Make sure your voicemail is recorded in a quiet environment and is professional, friendly, informative, and compelling.

Avoid making the mistake that so many executives make, which is to have someone else record the voicemail message. That screams, "I'm too busy for you."

An example of a professional voicemail message is:

Hello. You have reached the voicemail of Jo Smith of Smith Consulting. Please leave me a message. I will get back to you as soon as possible. You may also wish to send an email to jo.smith@smithcorp.com.

The general nature of media pitching is important. Even your voicemail pitch should follow certain guidelines to be effective.

BE BRIEF: Get to the point quickly. Lead with your strengths. Do not tell the whole story in the message; say enough so the reporter will call you back. On voicemail, the less said, the better. Here's an example:

Hi Dakota. It's Renee Nalas. I have a breaking news story about a merger in the pharmaceutical industry. My cell is XXX-XXX-XXXX. You can also reach me by email at XXX@XXXX.com. Again, my cell is XXX-XXX-XXXX.

BE MEMORABLE: The tone, volume, and pitch of your voice are as important as your message. Sound enthusiastic. Sound like you care about the story. Say one thing that will be memorable to the listener—speak in sound bites.

Remember to use as many media forms as possible. The more your target audience hears and sees your name, the more visibility, credibility, and validation you will receive.

MAKE IT EASY: Make it easy for the reporter or producer to call you back quickly. Leave your phone number twice, and state the numbers clearly and slowly. It is frustrating to have to replay the message. If you are working on a breaking news story, leave your mobile number. It is OK to say, "I can be reached until 9 p.m. today and after 7 a.m. tomorrow," to set parameters for times to be called back.

CALL AGAIN: Do not leave a second voicemail unless you have added information to share. Rather, call again until you speak to the person—when calling an office telephone only. If the reporter works from home or via a personal cell phone, try to reach that person via email before you call again. If you do not have any luck, put a day between your calls. This is media pitching, not stalking.

"Call anytime," said Cesca Antonelli, editor in chief at Bloomberg Industry Group. "We get tons and tons of unspecific emails. When you've got a good idea and you can tell us why something matters, that's the most important thing to us."

 🎙 *On Record PR Podcast: Bloomberg Industry Group Editor in Chief Cesca Antonelli Talks Legal, Tax, and Government News*

USING EMAIL TO PITCH EFFECTIVELY

Have you ever taken a vacation and come back to hundreds of emails? For many journalists, producers, and other media professionals, regardless of the medium, that is what their inboxes look like every day. How will your email stand out above the rest?

You can follow the general principles, but pitching by email is as uncertain as leaving a voicemail. It may or may not get through the spam filters at the other end, and if it does, the journalist may or may not read it. Here are some ways to keep your message out of the spam filters and junk boxes and get you into the journalists' minds.

THE SUBJECT IS *EVERYTHING*: The subject line is the first thing a recipient reads and sometimes the only thing. If it says, "Company Press Release," the journalist's mental response will probably be, "Oh great, another one." Instead use the catchy title of the release.

"Sometimes people get my attention with the subject line," said Erb. "There was a guy last year who was pitching for his boss to be on my podcast, and it worked. He referenced in his subject line a story that I had written. But it wasn't, 'I know you are interested in this.' It was a clever twist on something I had said. That caught my attention when I was skimming because I thought, 'Hey, that's my headline,' and then I read the article. The subject line should be thoughtful as well. I mean, it's part of the pitch. To me, it's like a headline."

Example: Jane Hess Provides Free Training to Assist with Ukrainian Visa Extensions in US

PERSONALIZE, PERSONALIZE, PERSONALIZE: Begin with "Dear [insert name of the reporter here]." Include a short paragraph that introduces the most important aspect of your story and why it should matter to that journalist and their readers, viewers, or listeners. At the close of your message, include *all* your contact information.

ONE IS ENOUGH: The general rule is to send your email to one reporter at a time and to only one reporter at each media outlet. It is frowned upon to bcc your full list of contacts with no personal message in the body copy. Pitch only one person at a particular media outlet unless you have a relationship with certain reporters and know they often work together. Generally, reporters collaborate, and most outlets conduct editorial meetings daily to determine who will cover what. If the story is not right for one reporter, that person may pass it on to someone else if it is right for the outlet.

KEEP IT SHORT: Keep your email as short as possible. Include a press release or other detailed information in the body of the email. Do not attach anything—especially if you are reaching out to the reporter for the first time. Many spam filters are programmed to eliminate attachments, including PDFs. You can include a link to information on your company's website; even then, spam filters may not let you through.

UNDERSTAND DEADLINES: Like calling a reporter, sending an email pitch on deadline is the worst time to reach out. You are adding to the clutter, noise, and frustration.

Do not make reporters work harder than necessary—it only raises red flags. Always be up front. Do not make a reporter dig for information.

Know where the line is and take pains not to cross it. Everything you send to the media must be truthful.

Send pitches on Tuesdays, the day most reporters open and respond (according to the 2022 Propel Media barometer).

Following these suggestions can help create a more positive response from reporters when pitching your story.

Common industry deadlines for daily newspapers are 3 p.m. Weekly magazines and newspapers often put their print edition to bed on Tuesdays or Wednesdays. For monthly publications call the desk and find out what week the deadlines fall on. For television and radio, the time and frequency of each show determine when the producers are in the office. Some morning show producers start their day at 2 a.m. and end at 10 a.m.

EMAIL SIGNATURES

An email signature is the block of text at the bottom of an email message that typically contains contact information, such as your name, title, company name, phone, mobile, email, and website address.

Using an email signature helps convey your brand and is akin to sending out your business card each time you email someone. It is also a sign that you are a professional and conveys legitimacy of your position and brand. If everyone in your establishment uses the same email signature style, you are presenting a sense of unity for your organization. This is usually the case with big companies, which control the employees' email signatures; however, some small- to midsize business professionals do not include any information after their names.

You can use your email signature to restate your company mission; link to a news article about you, your company, or something you have recently published; share accolades; and more. It is the easiest and least expensive way to reinforce what is going on with your company without being intrusive.

Example:
Sincerely,
Jo Smith
Chief Financial Officer
Smith & Smith Inc. 1234 Main Street | Ourtown, PA 12345
215.222.2222 | Jo.Smith@smithsmith.com | @Jo_Smith

Read my recent article in the *New York Times* on corporate finance issues and trends.

For those who work from virtual or home offices, it is OK to exclude your address. However, you may wish to consider a post office box.

SEEK MEDIA TRAINING: KNOW THE FOUR PS

Media training involves preparation, practice, planning, and performance. We call this the Four Ps. Each element is essential.

Media training teaches you how to interview, how to appear on television, how to communicate your message persuasively, and how to overcome physical and verbal roadblocks to effective communication. It is not a good idea to wing it.

1. PREPARATION

Representatives who plan to speak with reporters should be media trained. Most of us believe we can handle a media interview right out of school. If that is you, think again.

When I was on the Young Lawyers Division board for the Philadelphia Bar Association, I was invited to participate in a live debate against a

Washington, DC, Republican lobbyist on a topic I thought I knew a lot about—the Bill Clinton and Monica Lewinsky scandal. I was a last-minute substitute for someone well versed on the subject, and while I should have declined the interview, my ego got the better of me. Suffice it to say, I am glad we did not have YouTube, Vimeo, or social media at that time. The VCR tape supplied by the TV station has since been destroyed. I do not even want to use it for media training. It was that bad and goes down as one of my most embarrassing moments.

Less-than-ideal interactions with reporters will appear in stories and will quickly spread to many recipients over the internet.

Articles containing poorly worded statements, incomplete thoughts, or factually incorrect commentary can be and often are republished through email, blogs, and websites.

If you know how to communicate with the media effectively, you can generate a great deal of positive publicity for yourself and your company.

KNOW YOUR KEY MESSAGES: Formulate three key messages before speaking with the media. Determine the most important points that you wish to convey and write them down. This will help you prepare your thoughts and will lead to a more successful interview.

RESEARCH THE REPORTER: Before an interview, research the reporter with whom you will communicate so that you know what types of stories that person covers (hard-hitting or more conservative, for example).

ANTICIPATE QUESTIONS AND PREPARE ANSWERS: When you anticipate the questions the reporter will ask, you can plan your answers so they clearly and concisely convey your key messages. Practice how you will answer questions (do not memorize them) to make the interview more efficient. Be sure to include the questions you don't want to be asked and how you would answer those as well. That's usually what happens, especially on more controversial topics.

Here are some questions you can answer and practice (the second "P") if you are planning to reach out to media to be a subject-matter expert:

- What is the topic?
- What are the trends?
- What are your opinions (and why do they matter)?
- What are your predictions?
- What are the misconceptions?
- What questions do you want to answer?
- What questions do you dread?

2. PRACTICE

Use your questions and answers to practice mock interviews.

Have someone ask you all the questions you have drafted. Ask them to surprise you with questions you may not expect. If your topic is controversial, be prepared to answer the questions you dread.

If you will be interviewed for television, tape a mock interview. Play it back and critique yourself. Then ask others to do the same.

After each question, pause before you speak.

3. PLANNING

Know when, where, and how long your interview will last. If it is a telephone or recorded internet interview, be in a quiet location where you have privacy. Stand while you speak to better project your voice. If it is a radio or television interview on-site, arrive at least a half hour prior to the scheduled time.

If you are being interviewed in your office, ensure the room is in order, and store all sensitive or personal files out of sight.

If your interview is via Skype, Zoom, Teams, FaceTime, or another live video platform, adjust the height of your camera so you are looking straight ahead. If your camera is part of your computer, consider how your computer is positioned. You do not want to be looking down at a laptop screen. Have proper lighting and avoid distractions and interruptions. This means shutting off your telephone ringers; closing out of email so it doesn't ping; closing your door and putting a note on it saying, "Do not disturb"; and anything else that could cause a disruption during the interview.

If you expect to frequently participate in interviews and business meetings via live video platform, a high-quality microphone, webcam, ring lamp, and portable green screen may be valuable investments.

4. PERFORMANCE

When being interviewed, speak clearly and slowly in a conversational tone. Once you have made your point, pause and count to three. Wait for the interviewer to ask the next question, and don't be afraid of silence.

Silence is a tactic used to get you to talk, in the hopes of getting you to say something that you should not otherwise say. Silence could indicate that a reporter is planning the next question or transcribing what you have said. Regardless of the reason, do not feel pressured to fill the silence. Wait for the interviewer to proceed.

If you do your homework and keep these guidelines in mind, you will increase your chances of receiving the media attention you desire.

CHAPTER 4

WORKING WITH JOURNALISTS

"EVERYBODY WHO TALKS TO A NEWSPAPER HAS A MOTIVE.
THAT'S JUST A GIVEN. AND GOOD REPORTERS ALWAYS, REPEAT
ALWAYS, PROBE TO FIND OUT WHAT THAT MOTIVE IS."

—BEN BRADLEE

Be familiar with media terms before speaking with the media. Once you are familiar with these terms, have a conversation with the reporter to determine *their* definition of the terminology. People often use the phrase "off the record," but what does this mean to the reporter? That matters most.

MEDIA TERMINOLOGY: THE LANGUAGE OF JOURNALISTS

ON THE RECORD: "On the record" or "for the record" mean that what you say is fair game and may be included in the story with attribution to you. Therefore, your comments should be accurate, concise, and memorable. They are statements that you want the media to repeat.

"Any time you're talking to a reporter, you should assume that what you're saying is on the record until it's agreed by both parties that it's not," said Gina Passarella, the editor in chief of ALM Global, LLC.

 On Record PR Podcast: How Best to Work with Legal Media with Gina Passarella, Editor in Chief at ALM

OFF THE RECORD: Off-the-record comments should be avoided. My preference is that corporate representatives never make off-the-record comments because nothing is off the record. If you say it, then there is always a chance that it will end up published. "Off the record" means your name will not be attached to it (if the reporter agrees to this). If you do not want it researched or repeated, do not share it.

"If you say to a reporter as you're talking, 'Oh, this part I'm going to have off the record,' and you don't hear them say, 'OK, we're off the record,' that's not an agreement," ALM's Passarella said. "You need to stop before you continue talking with what you want to say off the record, and make sure that the reporter agrees, and then be clear about when you're going back on the record."

EMBARGO: An embargo usually entails providing an advance copy of an important press release or other information to the media with the explicit understanding that they will not release the story to the public until a specified date and time. When done right you maintain control of when the story breaks, and you give the media enough time to conduct research, gather quotes, and cover the story. If you offer an embargoed story to a sole reporter, never give that story to another reporter without the permission from the other. In addition, just because you offered it does not mean the reporter accepted the embargo. An embargo is an agreement between two parties.

Do not simply send a press release or email that says "Embargoed" at the top and expect the media to honor it. They have no duty to do so, and often they will not honor an embargo unless it is an explicit agreement with appropriate language to that effect.

You always risk a leak because there are no guarantees. A hungry member of the media could break an embargo without repercussion, or someone could have leaked the story. Know what you are dealing with and with whom.

Offering content under embargo does not mean you will retain control over the story. About embargoes, "I'll be honest, they're not a reporter's favorite," Passarella said. "Sometimes it does make things easier, but it can't stop us from being completely ethical and responsible in our coverage. Meaning, we can't not call the other side, and sometimes folks try to use the embargo to limit how much of the story we can report. We can't stop reporting the full story. We can work with you on timing."

EXCLUSIVE: An "exclusive" is when you give a particular media outlet the opportunity to be the only outlet to get the interview. Many journalists insist on exclusives.

SECOND-DAY STORY: A second-day story should turn hard news into a multifaceted story that blends the issues with human interest. It is an update with added information on a story that was previously told. A second-day story fills gaps in the original story, provides another angle, and shares expert opinion, data, or other new information.

FOR ATTRIBUTION: "For attribution" is like speaking on the record. The information the source provides is to be quoted and attributed to the person making the statement. The statement is usually followed by, "You can quote me on that."

NOT FOR ATTRIBUTION: The exact opposite of for attribution, "not for attribution" is when you provide the media with information that can be quoted or used, but that same information cannot be attributed to the source. Here the information or statement should be preceded by, "You cannot quote me on this." This can be a sticky way to present information to the media. If you do not want it attributed to you, then it is better left unsaid, like "off the record." If you do not wish to provide certain information, you might consider earning some points with the reporter by suggesting an alternative source.

ON BACKGROUND: According to a colleague who is an undercover investigative reporter, "on background" means that this reporter will not identify the source and will use the information provided by the source. "On background" can also mean that the information will not be attributed or used. It depends on the source's preference, which should be clarified between the source and the reporter.

ON DEEP BACKGROUND: When you say you are providing information to a reporter "on deep background," it means that the information is not for the public, but the reporter can use it to enhance the story or get additional information from other sources. This is another example of a situation in which it is better not to put it out there if you do not want it published.

HOW TO DECIDE ON TERMS

The general rule of thumb should be to believe that everything is on the record, fair game, quotable, available from someone else, attributable, and about the story (not you).

As a public relations professional, I advise clients to approach off-the-record or background conversations with care. Any degree of this type of interaction requires one vital element: trust between the journalist and the source.

When deciding whether to approach a journalist with an off-the-record or background tip, consider how well you know the reporter's beat. Will the information be of value to the reporter and their readers? Is the information valuable to the public overall?

Consider, too, how well you know the reporter as an individual. Have you shared sensitive information with that person before? Were you able to agree on terms of a previous conversation, and did the reporter and the publication uphold those terms?

That type of trust only can be developed over time. It also can be subject to the whims of an editor with whom you do not have a relationship. A reporter may have agreed not to use a source's name, but by the time the piece gets to the editors, they decide the agreement is not in the publication's best interest. Either the piece gets killed or the reporter must go back to the source and renegotiate terms.

Bottom line: If you are at all uncertain about the terms of a conversation, do not say anything you would not want to see printed on the front page or home page.

Even if both parties agree to go off the record or on background, the impressions and feelings created in the mind of the journalist by that conversation are long-lasting and can shape future coverage.

PERFORMANCE TIPS TO CONTROL YOUR MESSAGE

How you deliver information is as important as what you say.

BE CONCISE: When speaking to the media, be concise, and do not leave out vital information. You do not want a journalist to find out information on their own, then confront you with it when you are not prepared to answer questions.

DO NOT PANIC: If you are asked a question during an interview to which you do not know the answer, do not panic. Be honest and tell the reporter that you do not know the answer and that you would be happy to investigate it and get back to them. Do not make up an answer or wing it.

MANAGE YOUR EMOTIONS: Each situation is different and requires a level of emotional intelligence. If you are dealing with a sad set of circumstances, such as a death or a crisis, projecting empathy and understanding will help convey your message more effectively. If the situation requires you to play hardball and take a stance on a highly charged topic—such as a wrongful termination of an employee, discrimination, or unfair treatment—your demeanor should connote strength and fortitude. Keep your emotions in check during media interviews to deliver the most impactful message.

USE THE REPORTER'S NAME: When you speak with a journalist, use their first name, and try to relate to that person. The more you get to know reporters and become a resource for them, and the more they get to know you, the more likely they are to give you fair coverage.

NEVER SAY, "NO COMMENT": A corporate representative should never say, "No comment." When a spokesperson says this, it is perceived as an attempt to hide something or to avoid telling the truth. If something is confidential, then tell the interviewer you cannot divulge confidential information.

Effective alternatives to "No comment":
- Thank you for your question. What I can say is...
- It would be clearer if I first explained...
- I do not have all the facts to answer. I can say...
- That relates to a topic that we should address...
- If you're asking [rephrase], I can tell you...

NOTHING IS OFF THE RECORD: As I mentioned previously, there is no such thing as off the record. If you say it, then there is always a chance that it will end up published.

THE DOS AND DON'TS OF MEDIA RELATIONS

Now that we have covered media lingo and some rules of thumb, let's talk about additional dos and don'ts of media relations.

When communicating consistent messaging across multiple platforms, it can be helpful to adjust your delivery based on the medium in which it will appear and the audience to which it will be delivered. On their face, prepared, written statements are devoid of any outside factors that can cloud the messaging. When crafting a written statement, you can carefully deliberate on each word, but it may come across as flat or forced.

Alternatively, live comment requires much more attention to body language and vocal tone.

With live comment the viewer or listener interprets your words through the lens in which you present them. If your voice cracks with emotion or your eyes dart around the room, you are imparting additional meaning to your words, leaving room for varied interpretation.

Like you, reporters have pet peeves, norms, and unwritten rules. The following dos and don'ts will help keep you out of trouble and will gain goodwill among the journalists with whom you communicate during your career.

When communicating with the media, do:

- Be available and reachable
- Respect deadlines
- Be truthful and likable
- Avoid jargon
- Clarify misinformation
- Speak clearly
- Be responsive
- Use examples
- Use inflection, pitch, and tone
- Use verbal pace and pause
- Sit or stand comfortably
- Be calm and polite
- Be passionate and energetic
- Focus on your agenda
- Be clear and concise

When communicating with the media, do not:

- Get rattled
- Say, "No comment"
- Speak off the record
- Speculate or advise, if in regulated industries
- Fill dead air—remember, silence is an option
- Fidget
- Use negative statements
- Sound smug or arrogant
- Fill space with "um," "uh," "OK," "like," "you know," or "er"
- Nod your head after a question without verbally answering it

VIDEO, AUDIO, AND ONLINE INTERVIEWS

TELEVISION AND VIDEO-RECORDED INTERVIEWS

Video-recorded and live interviews require an additional set of guidelines. If you are interviewed for television:

WATCH THE PROGRAM SEVERAL TIMES BEFORE YOU ARE SCHEDULED TO APPEAR: Know the key players, their names, and the show's format.

CHOOSE YOUR MESSAGES WITH CARE: Television reaches a general consumer viewer, and morning news tends to have a larger female demographic. The producers have chosen to interview you based on a topic you have already agreed upon. Stick to that topic, or the reporter will cut you off and move on to the next segment.

STAY CALM, COOL, AND COLLECTED: Remember to be still. Do not sway back and forth or shake your feet. Take deep breaths. Pause between thoughts. Address the interviewer. Never look at the camera or monitors unless instructed otherwise. Keep your body language open and relaxed. Smile if the subject matter calls for a smile.

SPEAK IN SOUND BITES: Practice your topic in sound bites. Television is a great medium for short, quick sound bites that the viewers can remember. Television reporters are looking for short, to-the-point statements. You will rarely see a person talking for more than nine to ten seconds during a television story.

SPARE THE DETAILS: Most television stories run for less than ninety seconds. Television reporters are not looking for hours of drawn-out details. Be concise. Get to your point.

COUNT TWO SECONDS BEFORE ANSWERING: The slight pause before you answer will make your responses sound fresh and thoughtful.

USE FLAGS AND BRIDGES: Signal that a key point is coming up by flagging it with a phrase such as "The key point is..." or linking each answer to a positive message by using bridging phrases like "Let me put this in perspective" or "The real issue is..."

FLAGS AND BRIDGES:

- The key point is...
- Let's look at it from a broader perspective...
- The real issue is...
- Let's not lose sight of the underlying problem...
- There is another issue playing into this...
- The most important thing to remember is...
- I disagree. The opposite is true...

SPEAK IN PLAIN ENGLISH: The general television viewer speaks and reads at a seventh- to eighth-grade level. Speak in plain English to ensure that your message is clearly understood. Avoid industry jargon. Speak in lay terms so your audience understands you.

REMEMBER TO SAY YOUR COMPANY'S NAME: When you are first introduced, the reporter will mention your name only. The reporter will almost never mention the business. Mention your company when and if it is appropriate and comes naturally. Do not expect the company name to be included in the chyron (the text below the on-screen image). If it is, then that is the exception to the unwritten rule.

FOCUS ON YOUR OBJECTIVE: Do not get bogged down in statistics or lengthy explanations. Speak briefly, directly, and to the point. Correct any misstatements or misperceptions. Prepare key messages before speaking to the media. Know what your key messages are so that you get them across in your interview.

BEWARE OF INTERVIEWING TRAPS: Use your own words. Never repeat negative language or allow the reporter to put words in your mouth. Never lose your cool. Remember that nothing is really off the record.

PLAN FOR YOUR APPEARANCE: Follow the Four Ps.

DO NOT WEAR ALL WHITE: It glows and becomes the most noticeable thing on the television screen.

DO NOT WEAR ALL BLACK: It is too harsh. Black can absorb too much light. Other solid colors work better.

DO NOT WEAR BUSY PATTERNS: Thin stripes, busy tweeds, and prints produce distracting on-screen effects. This applies to ties and prints on shirts. Pastel shirts work well on TV.

DO NOT WEAR BRIGHT REDS: Reds bleed on camera and are distracting.

IF YOU'RE WEARING A SUIT JACKET, KEEP IT BUTTONED: Your suit will look more symmetrical, and you will appear more professional and polished. For men, this will keep your tie in place.

WEAR MAKEUP: If you do not wear powder on your nose, forehead, and face, you will look shiny, oily, and plastic. Make sure the powder makeup you use is the same color as your skin, not lighter or darker.

WATCH OTHER PEOPLE BEING INTERVIEWED: Watch others on television with the sound turned off to see which mannerisms are distracting to you. Avoid using any of the same distracting body language, facial expressions, or movements during an interview.

EAT WELL AND AVOID COFFEE OR MILK: Do not show up for the interview on an empty stomach. Your growling stomach will distract you. Coffee can make you jittery or nervous; milk can make your mouth feel gummy and will make it harder to talk. Drink plenty of water in advance of your interview.

"We prepared slide decks for the lawyers to reference regarding their appearance, what they should be wearing, voice pitch, voice speed, camera position, and lighting," said Susan DeLeva, former events manager at Dentons, a large law firm. "We want to make sure that we are doing anything and everything we possibly can so they are looking their best, presenting and showing the firm in the best light possible."

 On Record PR Podcast: Maximizing Opportunities in Virtual Event Planning with Susan DeLeva, Dentons

RADIO, PODCASTS, AND OTHER AUDIO INTERVIEWS

Like television, radio and other audio-only interviews have their own norms and idiosyncrasies. Close your eyes and listen to a radio news broadcast. Listen to interviews. Does the dialogue paint a visual picture with words and keep the message simple and to the point?

Keep the following guidelines in mind when seeking publicity on the radio, for podcasts, and via audio webinars:

DO YOUR HOMEWORK: Familiarize yourself with the reporters or the podcast host before pitching your story. Get to know the demographics of the listeners and any informational needs. Target only those outlets whose listeners are most likely to be interested in what you say.

MAKE YOURSELF KNOWN AS A SPOKESPERSON FOR AN ISSUE OR AN INDUSTRY: Because of the immediacy of radio and podcasts, interviewers have precious little time to hunt down sources when a story is breaking. If you readily come to mind, they are more likely to contact you. Share your profile and contact information in advance and connect on social media.

UNDERSTAND WHAT RADIO NEWS IS: Understand that your company's story or event will not be discussed on the radio unless it has true news value. If there is a human-interest angle, find out who should be contacted and whether the station covers human-interest stories. Podcasts are a much better platform for human-interest stories.

BE A GOOD GUEST: Know your material and answer the host's questions with the listeners in mind. Keep your answers brief. Provide enough information so the listeners will have learned something. Thank the host for having you as a guest and send a thank-you note after the interview.

ASK FOR A COPY: Many outlets will provide you with a digital copy of the program. Request information about copyrights and whether you may use the materials for your own purposes. If permissible use the audio recording on your website. Before you do, make sure it is of interest to your target audience.

REMEMBER THAT AUDIO LIVES ONLINE TOO: While your interview originally may have been for the radio, it is likely that the transcript or a summary of the interview will live online as a news story. Provide the reporter with relevant images if the outlet includes its audio interviews online.

PRINT AND DIGITAL PUBLICATIONS

Keep the following tips in mind when dealing specifically with print and digital media:

BE THOROUGH AND RESOURCEFUL: Print media can usually provide more space for a story than its television and radio counterparts, while digital media can allocate even more than print because they are not constrained by the written word and physical size of the publication. You can provide more information, photographs, or other visuals to promote your story in print and digital. Keep in mind that print publications have physical parameters (such as word counts and content per inch). The more interesting the story, the more likely the publication will cover it.

DO NOT ASK TO PROOF THE STORY BEFORE IT IS PUBLISHED: Reporters pride themselves on being accurate and professional, and they may find it offensive to have their work proofread. Permitting a source to review a story is taboo, and many editors have said they would fire a reporter for doing so. Fear not, however; many reporters will call to confirm names and facts before a piece is published.

REQUEST CORRECTIONS WISELY: It is not uncommon to spot errors in a story. Frequently, this is not the fault of the journalist; it typically happens during the editing process. When incorrect information affects the overall story, request corrections to information.

For example, if the story says, "In an interview on Monday," which took place on Tuesday, and the day of the week is not relevant or substantive, then leave the inaccuracy alone. If there is a substantive mistake, respectfully request that the error be corrected especially because the story will live online for a long time. Some publications will run a retraction or correction in the next print edition while others will only correct the mistake online.

When done right, media relations is a valuable tool to help companies gain credibility and establish validity. When the coverage is favorable, do not forget to share it as a media mention on your business's website and via social media. The more people who see it, the more likely it will enhance your credibility and business development efforts.

CHAPTER 5

MEDIA OUTREACH TOOLS

"WHAT I KNOW FOR SURE IS THAT SPEAKING YOUR TRUTH IS
THE MOST POWERFUL TOOL WE ALL HAVE."

—OPRAH WINFREY

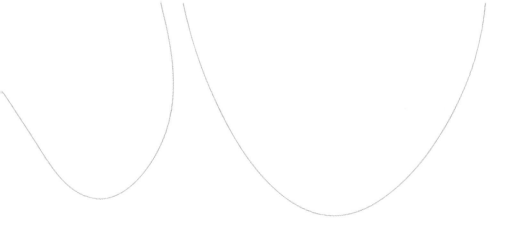

M edia relations begin with having credible expertise that is translatable and shareable with a public audience. Before you can begin to create relationships with members of the media, you must be perceived as a credible source of information who can add value to a conversation. This means that you or your company's key representatives need to have accessible, online content that establishes thought leadership and trust. Just because you think you're an expert doesn't mean that journalists will view you the same way. Make sure that your company biographies, LinkedIn biographies, and other online profiles are robust and speak to the expertise you wish to offer to journalists as a media source.

You also must develop relationships with journalists, editors, reporters, and media outlets. This is a foundational element and strategic process that may lead to media coverage in newspapers, magazines, television, radio, and online. Business journalists and editors often reach out directly to executives and to public relations professionals to help provide story ideas and to identify subject-matter experts and sources to interview for background information and visual imagery.

To receive media attention on relevant and timely stories, learn how to persuade the media to cover your topic. Pitching is the art of communicating a story idea, guest speaker, or news item to the media to gain publicity. To pitch your news and story ideas, become familiar with various media relations tools.

Protocol for media pitching is included in chapter 3. In this chapter, we explore various tools used to get your story told.

THE PITCH

As one who never developed much of a penchant for baseball, I'm not referring to a pitcher at the mound. Rather, in media relations, the pitch is used when you have news or a story to share, and you will focus on a select number of media outlets—your PML—to try to tell the story. I typically draft talking points and then call the reporter with whom I have an established relationship. There often are times when written communication is unnecessary and we do not recommend a press release, for whatever reason, and the story will be more compelling when shared directly.

For example, when a client had received Women's Business Enterprise National Council (WBENC) certification for which we drafted a press release, there was a more compelling story behind it to pitch.

This professional service company was only three years old, it was woman-owned, and its growth in revenue and number of professionals had increased inordinately. The company was doing wonderful things in the community and had an incredible growth story. We verbally pitched the story to a local industry reporter, and the reporter liked it. The reporter requested an in-person interview with our client. A growth story followed that featured the company and led to new business referrals from other professionals.

I should note that certifications such as minority-owned and women-owned are a fantastic way to establish credibility and to create news. Then, if the founder or company has a compelling story, there is more to pitch to media outlets.

Pitching people as experts to the media is a useful way to establish credibility around their products or services. For more than five years, we worked with a national accounting firm, Citrin Cooperman, managing their public relations. In addition to telling the company's news, we pitched various accountants and business advisers to raise awareness about the firm.

We pitched stories and thought leadership and secured placements in numerous publications, including various business journals, *Accounting*

Today, the *Philadelphia Inquirer, Huffington Post, USA Today, Real Estate Finance Journal, Risk Management Essentials, Auto Dealer Monthly*, GuideStar.org, and other daily and weekly publications.

THE PRESS RELEASE

The press release is a valuable media relations tool that you can use to strengthen your message via outreach. It also helps you develop your key messages and ensures that everyone in your organization agrees to the language you plan to use to communicate your message.

A press release is a concise tool most commonly provided to the media to generate public awareness and interest about a story or news. It should convey your story's who, what, when, where, why, and how. It is the written document designed to present the most newsworthy or attention-grabbing aspect of the story you are sharing.

Written in the third person, a press release should demonstrate the newsworthiness of a particular person, event, service, or story. When writing a press release, consider the audience. Some press releases are written as content for an organization's website. Others are written as a media pitching tool (which is what this chapter is about). If you plan to send the press release to the media, make sure that it is newsworthy.

To determine its newsworthiness, ask if the news matters to anyone outside of the company. Does this news make a difference? Would you read this if it did not involve your organization?

Situations that often warrant the use of a press release include:
- Awards and substantial rankings
- Certifications and other accomplishments
- Client or customer service initiatives
- Diversity, inclusion, and equity initiatives
- Economic impact stories
- Executive board appointments, election outcomes, and political appointments
- Executive hires, promotions, and management leadership changes
- Funding and financials announcements
- Initiative launches
- Marketing initiatives
- Mergers and acquisitions
- New business wins
- New office openings and corporate expansions
- New products, product lines, and service offerings
- Nonprofit involvement, corporate social responsibility (CSR), ESG, and sustainability campaigns
- Partnerships
- Presentations, seminars, and speaking engagements
- Publication of scholarly writings, white papers, and books
- Research and study results and trends backed with data

Research what your target media outlets are reporting on to confirm that they might be interested in your story.

If you decide you have something newsworthy, your press release should follow industry guidelines to help the media identify and clarify who you are, what your story is about, and how they can contact you for more information. Guidelines are included throughout this chapter.

USING THE PRESS RELEASE FOR BUSINESS DEVELOPMENT

Although the press release is typically used for media relations and press coverage, you can also use the press release to create a buzz, generate awareness, and develop business.

In addition to remaining top of mind with the media, communicate your messages to clients, customers, prospects, colleagues, friends, family, and referral sources. The more often these audiences hear your company's name, the more likely they will remember you when they need the services or products you provide.

Ways to leverage a press release in addition to using it as a media relations tool:

- Send the press release to current and prospective clients or customers, business partners, referral sources, family, and friends as "Company News" in an electronic alert or as part of a newsletter.
- Include the press release on your website.
- Share a link to the press release on social media.
- Send the press release to your employees and encourage them to pass the news along to their contacts.
- Include copies of your more important press releases in your company's press kit, newsletters, and leave behinds.
- Have extra copies of your press releases available to attendees of your seminars and at your trade show booths when relevant.

Notwithstanding the type of news, a press release can be used in many ways as a business development tool to increase awareness of your organization and its offerings, communicate your services, differentiate your organization from competitors, retain current clients, and generate new business.

WRITING A PRESS RELEASE

Many factors go into writing a good press release and will influence the amount and type of coverage your news will receive. Follow industry standards so your communications are effective.

First, follow a style guide.

Choose a source for spelling conventions. For this book, we chose *Merriam-Webster's Collegiate Dictionary*.

Also choose a source for style conventions.

Two of the most common stylebooks used for writing public relations materials are the *Chicago Manual of Style* (CMoS) and the *Associated Press Stylebook* (AP). Each provides recommendations for preferred writing styles.

For this book, we predominantly followed CMoS, 17th edition; however, I chose between the two styles where I found one to be more conversational in tone than the other.

At my company we follow *AP Stylebook* practices for drafting, editing, and proofreading all written copy for clients. You can subscribe to it at apstylebook.com.

For example:

- In press releases, we do not refer to individuals in the second mention as "Mr.," "Mrs.," or "Ms." This should be consistent in all press releases and media content.
- We use punctuation that is consistent with AP style.
- When referring to a city and/or state, we defer to the style noted in the guide.

While there are thousands of rules in the guide, I am only noting a few here.

INCLUDE THE DATE AND TIME YOUR NEWS IS TO BE RELEASED:
The recipient of your press release needs to understand the time sensitivity of your news. Tell the reporter when it is OK to disseminate the information. Common language to provide this information includes:

FOR IMMEDIATE RELEASE
FOR RELEASE BEFORE [DATE]
FOR RELEASE AFTER [DATE]

This language should appear at the top of the press release and be all caps, underlined, or bold. Include a dateline in bold. The dateline is listed at the beginning of the first paragraph with the city, state abbreviation, and date of the news's origin.

Datelines for small businesses will likely be where the business is located; however, if the organization's news relates to a different location, and you want media coverage where the matter is taking place, use that city and state in the dateline. The same holds true for big companies; if your news is relevant to an individual office, change the dateline in the press release when sending it to media outlets in different cities and states to convey relevance.

STATE ABBREVIATIONS: The *AP Stylebook* states that the names of the fifty states should be spelled out when used in the body of a story, whether standing alone or in conjunction with a city, town, village, or military base.

INCLUDE CONTACT INFORMATION: It is frustrating to a reporter or editor to receive an interesting press release without contact information. When sending a press release via email, place the contact's name, business phone number, cell phone number, and email address at the top of the message.

INCLUDE AN ATTENTION-GRABBING HEADLINE: An attention-grabbing headline is imperative. The headline must entice the recipients to read your release and should not be quirky or silly.

To write better headlines, read the headlines featured in newspapers, magazines, blogs, and any other media outlets you are trying to target. Headlines are meant to tell the story and catch the reader's attention in a few short words.

For example, you announce that Jane Doe is joining the Philadelphia office of XYZ Company as the chief financial officer.

The headline should read: "Jane Doe Joins XYZ Company as CFO in Philadelphia."

TAILOR THE HEADLINE TO THE OUTLET: Tailor your headline to each media outlet so each will know why your story pertains to it or its audience.

Assume Jane Doe is a member of the CFO Leadership Council. The release sent to the editor of its internal newsletter or member publication should have a headline reading:

CFO Leadership Council Member Jane Doe Joins XYZ Company as Chief Financial Officer

The same holds true for alumni publications, newspapers from the town where Jane Doe resides, and other affinity organizations such as diversity and ethnic publications.

INCLUDE A SUBHEADLINE TO ADD VALUE: A subheadline can be useful when used properly. In a press release, it provides an opportunity for you to incorporate your news angle and further catch the reporter's attention without taking away from the headline.

In the case of Jane Doe, assume she left another prominent national company, ABC Company. The subheadline could read: "Doe Leaves ABC Company to Lead Newly Reorganized Financial Leadership Team."

PROVIDE THE NEWS VALUE: Tie your press release topic into the news. Come up with story angles that will be interesting for reporters; tell them why their readers will care about this information and how the story will benefit their audience.

If your press release is informational, keep it short.

For example, if you are pitching your local business journal, the news must be valuable to business readers. Ask why a reader would care about your story. Use your answer to craft a sentence or two about the news value of your story and how it relates to the business industry regionally.

SUMMARIZE THE RELEASE IN THE FIRST PARAGRAPH: Also known as the press release lead, the first paragraph should tell the recipient what the release is about. Get to the point. The first paragraph should answer who, what, when, where, and why. If the reporter is crunched for time, they can include the basics of your story in a news item. Include figures to emphasize the size of the deal, increase in revenue, or any other quantifiable fact you have included in the press release. Many local newspapers include blurbs about local business news without going into detail. If the first paragraph of your press release says, "Jane Doe joined XYZ Company as chief financial officer. She will work from the company's headquarters in Philadelphia," and that is all that the outlet picks up, then you have told the entire story.

KEEP IT SHORT AND CONCISE: Typically, a press release should be one page. Stick to the facts and use only enough words to tell your story. Print publications have space restrictions and may need to cut off the last paragraph. Make sure you have the most essential information first, followed by more details that may be interesting but are not crucial. Always write clearly, using proper grammar and spelling.

It is good practice to draft the press release one way to be shared with the media and to expound on the information on the version that is added to your website and shared with your audience via social media and other means. The website version of your press release should include additional keywords and phrases, links to internal and external content, internal links of related news, and relevant information about your business to enhance the search engine optimization value (the SEO score) of the content.

AVOID JARGON AND EXCESSIVE ADJECTIVES: The reader is not looking for fluff, and jargon is distracting. Avoid unnecessary adjectives, fancy language, overstated claims, or superfluous expressions, such as "superior services" or "extremely experienced and qualified." Such language raises red flags as fluff with a reporter.

CHECK YOUR FACTS: Confirm that your information is correct. If you have issued your press release and you made a mistake, or if the facts change along the way, let the reporter know and ask for a change.

INCLUDE A QUOTE: Quotes help to make the press release more personal and add value to the tool. Some publications will never run quotes unless they have been verified by a reporter or editor at the publication. This holds true for most national print publications. However, many local newspapers will run your press release verbatim.

Continuing with the Jane Doe story, a valuable quote would come from the hiring or managing partner of XYZ Company explaining why Jane was hired, the value she brings to the organization, and how this benefits the organization's clients and/or positions the organization for future success.

USE NAMES IN YOUR RELEASE: Include the most important people in your news story. Write out the person's full name and title on the first reference in the release. For the online version, link to the individual's profile.

Use Jane Doe on first reference. After that, Jane Doe is referred to by last name only: Doe. Do not use Ms. Doe or Mrs. Doe or Jane. Not including a prefix is extremely uncomfortable for some executives and is something our team has had to explain repeatedly.

Using only the last name is not the case when writing biographies for your company's website or client communications. Other than in media communications such as press releases, name conventions depend on your company's culture, the types of clients or customers you serve, and how previous materials have been written (for consistency).

INCLUDE A BOILERPLATE: A boilerplate is the standard block of text used at the end of the press release. Your boilerplate should be consistent and used for all press releases. It should be reviewed and, if necessary, updated at least quarterly. The boilerplate should contain a brief description of your organization and should always be included in press releases sent to the media or issued on newswires. On the other hand, it is the company's preference as to whether the boilerplates are included on the website version of the release. Some prefer it for consistency and SEO, while others do not.

XYZ Company's boilerplate might read:

XYZ Company is one of the nation's leading software companies, transforming clients' operations and technology models for the digital era. Our unique approach helps clients build and run more innovative and efficient businesses. Headquartered in Philadelphia, XYZ Company is consistently listed among the most admired companies in the United States. Learn how XYZ Company helps clients at www.xyzcompany.com or follow us @ XYZCompany.

INDICATE THAT THERE ARE NO MORE PAGES TO THE RELEASE: After the main body of the release and boilerplate, skip a line and in the center type "#####." This end notation lets the reporter know that there are no more pages to the release when printed. It is an archaic but often necessary convention.

RESEARCH THE INTENDED RECIPIENT OF YOUR PRESS RELEASE:
Before sending a press release to the media, research the reporter or editor you are targeting. Make sure the reporter or editor is the correct individual to receive the release. You can go to the outlet's website, use a paid media database source, or pick up the phone and call the publication to ask.

PRESS RELEASE CHECKLIST

The following checklist will help you identify all elements needed for an effective press release:

- Dateline and release line
- Contact information
- Headline
- Subheadline (optional)
- Personalized information for each media outlet
- Who
- What
- When
- Where
- Why
- How
- Quote (optional)
- Boilerplate
- End notation

Your press releases should be newsworthy and different from your competition. If you follow the strategies and tactics provided here, get ready to see some impressive results.

WIRE DISTRIBUTION OF A PRESS RELEASE

Once you know how to pitch the media and put the media to work for you, you can use additional tools, such as wire services, strategically.

Wire services, both paid and free, serve the purpose of providing the media with information they have requested on certain topics. However, unless you are a large organization or your news is extraordinary, using a national wire service is not likely to get your story covered. Wire services will help get your company's story out online and onto websites that curate their news from the wires.

Wire services include:
- Associated Press (ap.org)
- Black PR Wire (blackprwire.com)
- Business Wire (businesswire.com)
- eReleases (ereleases.com)
- GlobeNewswire (globenewswire.com)
- Hispanic PR Wire (hispanicprwire.com)
- Legal Newswire (law.com/legalnewswire)
- PR Newswire (prnewswire.com) by Cision
- PR Web (prweb.com) by Cision
- Reuters (Reuters.com)

THE MEDIA PHOTO

Include a high-resolution photo (300 dpi or higher) with your press release to add greater impact and news value to your story, not only for the readers but also for the editor when deciding which stories to cover. If you have a professional photo of a person or event that you can attach to a release, it will help your chances of getting coverage.

Include photos that illustrate the news in your press release for visual effects. A press release with a photo attached is four times more likely to be read. Smaller, local publications like to receive photos with press releases because it enables them to publish photos without having to send a photographer or reporter to take pictures. Larger publications also like to receive photos because, in addition to adding interest to a story, photos help the writer authenticate the story or event.

Headshots highlight the people featured in a news story. Professional, up-to-date headshots should be kept on file. They have a shelf life of four to eight years (depending on how often you change your hairstyle). If your headshot is more than eight years old, it is time to ante up and get a new one.

A photo shoot can be a fruitless venture if you are not properly prepared. Have a professional do your makeup and hair. Show expression:

let your eyes do the talking. Smile when it is appropriate. Use your body language to express your sentiment. Look into the camera. The focus is on you, not on what you are wearing. Dress in simple, solid-colored clothing. Avoid patterns or wearing all one color. Layering with a collared shirt or jacket allows you to look professional and vary your look easily from shot to shot.

Expect that the shoot will take thirty minutes to an hour. Allow plenty of time so that you are not rushed or stressed. Remember that the photographer is a professional. This person will use their skills and experience to create the best photos for your needs. Practice your facial expressions (smile, no smile, teeth showing, serious, empathetic) in a mirror. Have several shirts and jacket options and bring them all with you on the day of the shoot. Get plenty of sleep the night before the shoot. Relax and have fun. Your picture will reflect that.

When it comes time for you to get your headshot taken, remember that it does not have to be a stressful undertaking. Arrive prepared and be yourself. If you do your part, the professionals involved can easily capture pleasing visuals.

SUBMITTING PHOTOS TO THE MEDIA

As already indicated, a headshot illustrates one person. However, it often is necessary to send a photo that captures an event or illustrates your story. When you send event photos, make sure you know the editors' preferences. Some editors would rather receive candid shots taken in the style of photojournalism. Other publications—especially trade journals and business journals—will want you to send the standard business photos.

GIVE YOUR PHOTO A DESCRIPTIVE NAME: When sending a digital photo, make sure the name of the image depicts exactly who or what it is. If you are sending a headshot of Jane Doe, name the photo "JaneDoe_XYZCompany." If you send IMG_001, there is no way to identify that

IMG_001 is a photo of Jane Doe, especially if the photo is forwarded to another person at the publication.

INCLUDE A DESCRIPTIVE CAPTION: Include a descriptive photo caption following the boilerplate. Include the subject of the photo, the names and titles of the people in the photo, and where it was taken. Give attribution to the professional photographer. Since we read from left to right, your photo caption should (if depicting people) state, "From L to R: [Name 1], [Name 2], [Name 3]," and so on. "Photo credit: [Name of photographer]."

In addition, determine the publication's size requirement for digital images. Most publications require 300 dpi, 5″ by 7″ JPEG files. Use the name of your company, event, or the person pictured to save the photo. Make sure the editor or reporter accepts attachments, as many email filters do not.

If your office can upload photos to the corporate website, include a link to the photo page at the end of your press releases. This is a useful way to share captioned photos with the media. It allows them to choose which photos best illustrate the story. They should be given the choice to download high- or low-resolution copies of the images for use with their publications.

Use online file-sharing tools like Dropbox or WeTransfer when possible. It is also possible to send photo options using photo galleries like Flickr, iCloud, Google Photos, Shutterfly, SmugMug, 500px (used by professional photographers), Facebook, Amazon Photos, or Photobucket. Although the media cannot always download a digital file from these sites, they can tell you which photos they would like you to send. This form of communication should be used sparingly as it adds more work for the reporter. If you have a good relationship, the reporter will likely want to look at the photos and make their own choices. Take the time to include information about each photo (names, location, date).

THE BACKGROUNDER

A corporate backgrounder is an informational document that provides in-depth background material about a company, person, place, issue, or story.

The hallmarks of a good backgrounder are accuracy and comprehensiveness. Backgrounders serve to introduce the organization, an executive, a news item, experts, service offerings, and the management team. They also make it clear why you are contacting members of the media.

Public relations practitioners use backgrounders to provide journalists with enough information on a subject to conduct a thoughtful and intelligent interview. They provide supplemental information to the press release, which needs to be short and succinct.

Usually not more than one to three pages, the backgrounder answers anticipated questions about the subject. The more information, the more prepared you will be when the media calls. This is especially true when dealing with complex issues and matters that have been the focus of media scrutiny. The backgrounder, when used, often accompanies a press release.

When drafting a corporate backgrounder:

REPEAT YOUR CONCISE STATEMENT OF THE ISSUE OR EVENT: The statement of the issue or event that is the subject of your press release should be repeated as your opening.

PROVIDE A HISTORICAL OVERVIEW: Follow the opening with a historical overview. Keep it tight and organize it either chronologically or in another order that will make sense to the reader. Describe the evolution—give it perspective. How did it start, and what were the major events leading up to its conclusion or resolution?

INCLUDE A MISSION AND VISION WHEN RELEVANT: These help the reader to understand the background about an organization and are especially important for nonprofit organizations and government-funded initiatives.

CITE YOUR SOURCES: If you refer to other materials, such as books, websites, or news items, cite your sources.

INCLUDE OTHER THOUGHT LEADERS: A backgrounder is used to provide that: background. Such information also includes additional sources for a complete story, such as the company's spokesperson, industry experts, and others who might add depth to the reporter's story.

PROVIDE RELEVANCY: Explain why the issues you highlighted are relevant today. Ask, "What is the significance? Why does this matter today? Who cares?" Then back up your relevancy statement with facts.

INCLUDE THE EXECUTIVE'S EXPERIENCE: Rather than clutter the press release with a full-page biography about Jane Doe, include her full biography in the backgrounder. This is a helpful place to list Doe's involvement in other situations that add depth to the story.

INCLUDE A CORPORATE OVERVIEW: Include an overview of your company. No matter the size of your organization, there is an organization behind you, even if you are a sole proprietor. Include an overview to provide perspective, even if it is identical to your website's about us information.

ORGANIZE YOUR BACKGROUNDER WITH SUBHEADINGS: Use subheadings where appropriate to organize your information and make it easier to read. Based on the tips provided here, your subheadings should include issues, historical overview, relevancy and facts, additional sources or commentators, executive biographies, and a company overview.

THE OPINION EDITORIAL (OP-ED)

Op-eds and letters to the editor (the next topic) should be used sparingly. They are highly effective communication tools.

An opinion editorial (op-ed) is used to express an opinion. It is an underutilized and powerful way to publish your opinion and demonstrate depth of knowledge on a particular topic. In this way you can be positioned as a thought leader in your area of expertise and as one who is willing to take a stand.

An op-ed is in the opinion pages of a newspaper, magazine, website, or blog.

The op-ed submissions that get published deal with often-controversial topics of current interest and take a stand on the issues addressed. It is your opinion, so make it stick.

Be careful if your op-ed deals with a topic that is directly related to your business, such as ongoing litigation or a pending transaction.

Because newspapers get countless op-ed submissions, getting one published can be difficult. When writing an op-ed, follow these guidelines to increase the odds that yours will get published.

BE OPINIONATED: The more rare or controversial your opinion, the more likely the op-ed will be published.

WRITE ABOUT ONE THING: If you cannot sum up your ideas in the headline, then it is not the best topic to choose for an op-ed.

WRITE IN THE ACTIVE VOICE: It is easier to read.

MAKE A UNIQUE POINT: Before you submit your op-ed, research what the publication has recently published on the topic. Do not repeat what others already have said.

KEEP IT TO AROUND SEVEN HUNDRED WORDS: Typically, op-eds should be about seven hundred words, although they can be shorter or longer, depending on the outlet. Keep in mind that print publications have limited space, and most of the time, editors will not take the time to cut an op-ed down. You can determine the exact parameters by obtaining the submission guidelines.

STAY FOCUSED: Do not derail the train by trying to provide too much backup. It is the short, concise opinions that are the most memorable.

BE TIMELY: If you are writing about an event in today's news, submit your opinion timely—either on the same day or a couple of days later. Op-eds deal with what is happening in the here and now.

CONNECT LOCALLY: Use the local approach when writing for a newspaper within your community. Tie your commentary to local events and include your place of residence and why the issue matters to you. Many lobbyists and special-interest groups write op-eds as part of their regular outreach strategy. Local papers are more likely to publish a column by a local author than by a lobbyist.

KNOW YOUR AUDIENCE: Choose the right publication for your op-ed. Submit your piece to only one outlet. Ask who is reading the publication and why you want them to read what you must say. If you are a local consumer-facing business, stick to the local newspapers. More people in your target demographic read them than the *New York Times* and the *Wall Street Journal*. Conversely, if you serve as a more specialized audience, you may be better served with an article in a targeted trade publication.

DEFINE WHO CARES: Explain why the publication's readers will care about your issue and opinion. As with all forms of public commentary, make sure the readers are engaged and have a stake in your message, as you will certainly want to share your op-ed on social media as well.

LETTERS TO THE EDITOR

A letter to the editor, also known as commentary, is another great way to reach out to the media and to demonstrate your thought leadership. It is a way to share your opinion, educate the public about the issues, applaud someone for doing the right thing, or criticize policies. A well-written, well-timed letter to the editor can shift public opinion, influence policy, and receive substantial media attention.

Letters to the editor date back many years. The *New York Times* has been receiving them since it was founded in 1851. Today the *Times* receives more than one thousand letters per day from readers all over the world.

Letters to the editor should be inspired by stories that touch on subjects that relate to your business, industry, or passions.

Whether it is a story about human rights, a study that reveals the prevalence of racial disparity in a particular type of business or industry, a legislative issue, or an article about governmental policies—there is always something to which you can respond.

When submitting a letter to the editor, review the publication's policies and guidelines. Many have word count limitations and submission requirements that you must follow.

Editors prefer to publish timely, concise letters that respond to an article, editorial, or other letters that appeared in the publication and are relevant to issues of local or regional importance. If you are responding to a weekly periodical, give yourself no more than forty-eight hours, depending on its print cycle.

Your letter must stand on its own. Open your letter with a strong statement that comments on the original topic. Your opening comments can take issue with a statement made by the journalist, agree with and support a critical point, clarify a comment made by someone who was interviewed for the original story, add discussion points about something readers would need to know, disagree with an editorial position, introduce a little-known fact or issue related to a subject, or point out an error or misrepresentation in an article. Be careful about accuracy and avoid personal attacks.

The letter must remain short and focused. Close with the thought you most want readers to remember.

Ask a colleague to review your letter to be sure your writing is clear, that you are getting your point across, and that there are no grammatical or spelling errors.

Include your full name, the company for which you work (if relevant), and your address, cell phone number, and email address. Editors are wary of fake letters or those written to promote a product or company. Most will contact you to verify that you wrote your letter and that you are providing the paper with permission to publish it.

Submit letters by email to the editor of the publication or use the outlet's website submission form to send your letter.

To write effective letters to the editor, avoid jargon. Write with passion and from your heart. Remain focused on a single topic. Pick your battles wisely. Use verifiable data to illustrate your points. Anticipate that your letter will be shortened. Lead with your most poignant points. Include a strong message in each paragraph. Use examples that relate to readers, and do not include a litany of self-serving commentary.

The letters to the editor section is one of the most frequently read sections of the newspaper and is always published in the editorial section. When done right, your letter to the editor will afford you a great deal of credibility and recognition from those you wish to influence.

ADVERTORIAL

There are times when media outlets will not run a story or commentary and the information is too important not to share with your target audience. When this happens, there is an option to publish an advertorial, which is akin to an advertisement or sponsored content.

An advertorial is a paid placement of a written message to explain, clarify, apologize, thank, share, or otherwise communicate with a particular audience. It is written in the style of an editorial or objective journalistic article or as a letter to the readers.

Just like an advertisement, an advertorial is a paid placement; however, the advertorial allows you to author a story or share a letter to help the reader better understand your product or services.

The benefits of advertorials are that you control the message and the medium and that they support brand awareness. Advertorials often are viewed as more trustworthy than an advertisement. The content can be shared just like any other articles on social media. Advertorials can include a call to action, which can generate both leads and conversions.

QUESTIONS AND ANSWERS (FREQUENTLY ASKED QUESTIONS OR FAQS)

You can use questions and answers, also known as FAQs, in myriad ways within your public relations efforts. One way is to draft frequently asked questions and their answers to provide to members of the media.

FAQs can be used to optimize your website or to prepare you and other members of your organization for questions the media might ask in specific situations.

Keep a notebook next to your phone and write down frequent questions you are asked about your company or its products or services. Draft your answer so that when a reporter interviews you, your answers are organized and available.

CALENDAR LISTING

A calendar listing is a tool used to get a free listing of an event or program mentioned by media outlets. It provides information for upcoming events relevant to their audience. Calendar listings are issued in advance of an event. They should increase awareness and attendance. If your event is by invitation only, a calendar listing should not be used.

Determine by when and to whom your listings should be sent. There usually is a calendar or events editor assigned to this information for print publications. Television and radio stations usually accept calendar listings via their websites only.

If you want the calendar listing in a monthly print publication, you may need to provide it as early as ninety days in advance. Weeklies often require two to three weeks, and dailies usually require at least one week's notice. Many websites provide the ability to upload the information yourself and, once approved (usually within twenty-four hours), will post your listing online.

Like press releases and other publicly shared media information, the calendar listing must include the who, what, when, where, and why.

MEDIA ADVISORY

A media advisory is most often used to entice members of the press to attend an upcoming event. Much shorter than a press release, a media advisory covers who, what, when, where, and why. Unlike a press release, a media advisory is not meant to be a pseudo news story. It should be a succinctly written enticement like a save-the-date notice, which alerts reporters and editors to a future event or story opportunity.

Media advisories are typically sent out in advance of a press conference.

Your media advisory is meant to persuade reporters to attend. It should not provide so much information that a reporter could write the story without showing up. Keep the advisory to one page, and do not include too many details. It is customary practice to lead with an engaging headline (and possibly a subheadline). Conclude the advisory with the same boilerplate you would place at the end of a press release.

For planned events, send your advisory approximately four weeks in advance of the event so reporters can plan to attend, and always keep the advisory to one page. Be sure to conduct research to ensure that the advisory is sent to the appropriate reporters.

If it is a breaking story, you may only have hours to issue the media advisory. Timing will always depend on the issue.

For longer-lead invitations, resend the advisory the day before the event.

If there will be a photo opportunity, a live video feed, or other visual opportunities, include that information in your advisory.

Issue your advisory in the body of the email, not as an attachment.

Include directions and information about parking, refreshments, and accommodations, then follow up with a phone call as the event date approaches.

A media advisory should be punchy and enticing. You want to convince the press to attend your event or to cover your story. Keep it short and let them know why your story is worthy of attention.

FACT SHEET

A fact sheet is like a backgrounder. It provides data and facts that support the news you are sharing with the media. The fact sheet must be short and concise.

Though fact sheets can be standalone, they are more commonly submitted along with a press release or media kit. Include the basic who, what, when, where, why, and how; a contact name; information; and a subject line or title.

A well-written fact sheet will include data important to the end consumer of the information.

When we handled the grand opening of the Pennsylvania Biotechnology Center in Bucks County, Pennsylvania, we invited press. The fact sheet included the following:
- Date, time, and location of the opening
- Facility details
- Investment
- Space allocations and usage
- Square footage
- Amenities
- Equipment

- The number of new jobs offered
- Data from an economic impact report
- Discoveries by the scientists who will work in the biotech center
- Government officials' involvement
- Business partners (architects, builders, interior designers, banks)
- Certifications and more

PRESS KIT

A press kit, also known as a media kit, is a useful tool in public relations. It is a collection of information about your organization, your news story, the individuals, the issues, and the experts who can discuss the matters that affect you and your target audience. It should be used to provide more details to the media, not as a primary tool to pitch to the media.

Press kits save time and improve accuracy by providing the information that journalists need for their reports.

What to include in your press kit:
- Biographies of key business leaders
- Copies of relevant news clippings and reprints
- Fact sheets
- Corporate backgrounder
- Mission statement
- Photos
- Q&As
- Recent press releases

When using a press kit as a media tool, do the following:

INCLUDE A COVER LETTER: Indicate what is included in the kit and whom to contact for additional information.

KEEP PRESS KITS ON HAND: Press kits will not help you if you do not distribute them. Have press kits available at the office, at trade shows, at community events, and at relevant company events. Make your press kit readily available to each news outlet you encounter. Make a note on your website that press kits are always available to members of the media. Provide an email link for media requests, or make the press kit available on your website as a downloadable file.

USE BRANDED MATERIALS: Use corporate letterhead and other branded collateral for each element of the press kit. It is professional and ensures that your contact information and corporate brand is clearly associated with the press kit.

KEEP IT CURRENT: Update your press kit frequently by including current press releases and news coverage. Publications want the latest, most up-to-date information about your organization.

As with all corporate public relations efforts, identify what you want to accomplish. Once you know your goal, you can choose the media outreach tools that will accomplish your objectives. They are not all meant to be used at the same time, and not every tool is right for every message.

Choose strategically.

CHAPTER 6

WRITING AND SPEAKING FOR THOUGHT LEADERSHIP

"THOUGHT LEADERSHIP IS WHEN A LEADER'S THOUGHTS ARE
BEING USED BY LEADERS TO LEAD OTHERS."

—ONYI ANYADO

Writing and public speaking often feel daunting. When business-people are told they should draft an article or speak on a particular topic, they often say they are too busy, do not have time, do not know what to write or speak about, or that their audience is not looking for their services online. Conversely, I have had the experience of working with professionals who love to write or speak and understand the value of thought leadership.

If you have something to say and you want to say it to a particular audience as an authority on the matter, writing and speaking are effective tools for getting your point across.

LONG- AND SHORT-FORM CONTENT

Create an arsenal of articles, blogs, and other types of content in short and long lengths. Google algorithms indicate that longer-form content (more than two thousand words) performs better for SEO than shorter content. Google changes its algorithms regularly. Your copy still should focus on a single message.

Clear and concise copy improves the overall comprehension and appearance of your written materials and boosts exposure, message recall, and the overall efficiency of your public relations endeavors.

Leslie Richards, chief innovation officer at Furia Rubel Communications, explains:

> What has happened in search is exciting and good news for humans. Google is focused on natural language processing as part of its understanding of content online. If you want to think about how Google functions, think of it more as artificial intelligence, with search being just one component. As Google becomes increasingly sophisticated, it can understand the context in which your content exists. It understands not only the page that it is reading, but all the other pages attached to that page and whether the content on that page seems related to the rest of the site. It determines whether the website is an authoritative source for the topic.

 🎙 *On Record PR Podcast: Planning for Digital Marketing in 2021, with Leslie Richards, CIO of Furia Rubel Communications*

Besides your main story, you might repackage your content as sidebars, lists, related stories, freestanding vignettes, fun facts, or trivia. Include visuals whenever possible.

Paragraph length is among the most important signals you send to readers about how easy and interesting your copy is to read. If your paragraphs are too dense, the information appears cumbersome and uninviting. If they are all the same length, the information can appear boring.

Vary the lengths of your paragraphs to create a sound rhythm for your writings. Shorter is better. Try to keep your paragraphs to three sentences, and keep in mind that single-sentence paragraphs are acceptable.

EMBRACE EDITORIAL GUIDELINES

When writing for a print publication, read and review several previous editions to get a feel for the types of articles it typically includes.

Research the publisher's editorial guidelines (also known as writers' guidelines) for contributing authors. Editorial guidelines are usually on the publications' websites. Follow those guidelines to refine your article before submitting it for consideration.

Editorial guidelines commonly address the length of article: the minimum and maximum word count (an optimum number of words per article might also be listed); the preferred format of articles for submission; topics accepted by the publication; copyrights; the use of illustrations and images; the editorial style, such as compliance with the *Associated Press Stylebook* for abbreviations, capitalization, grammar, punctuation, and spelling; the inclusion of an author's biography and headshot; compensation (if any); query and submission requirements; and editorial calendars, which include topics, themes, article types, and required submission dates broken down by publication date.

An editorial calendar is a schedule of topics to be covered by a publication over time or to be written about by your company for articles, blogs, newsletters, social media posts, and so on.

Comply with the editorial guidelines to maximize your chances of having the article accepted. If you are not sure about something, contact the editor and ask. It is a fantastic way to start a conversation and to offer yourself as available for commentary on similar issues while getting the required editorial information to submit your article.

TYPES OF WRITING

There are several types of writing that you can use to generate a buzz about you and your expertise. They include articles, blogs, FAQs, tip sheets, books, and white papers.

THE AUTHORITATIVE ARTICLE OR BLOG

Writing and publishing authoritative articles or blogs are some of the easiest and most effective ways to garner valuable publicity—especially if you like to write. When an article is published, you establish credibility with your target audience. It positions you as a thought leader without your having to say, "Hey, look at me. I'm an expert on this topic."

Authoritative articles should highlight your expertise and the industries or audiences you serve.

Many media outlets accept well-written, timely, and relevant authoritative articles and others on which you can syndicate your writings.

American Lawyer Media, for instance, publishes a variety of legal trade periodicals categorized by region, size of the law firm, audience (i.e., general counsel), law practice management topics (such as technology), and other areas of interest for law firms. If lawyers are seeking to grow their business through lawyer referrals, articles about trends and updates in their areas of practice are of value.

Various print and online outlets publish authoritative content for syndication. They also are known as content aggregators.

Consider leveraging free or paid syndication services such as Quora, Medium, SlideShare, Reddit, Outbrain, Tumblr, and Taboola. These syndication platforms are user targeted and read by decision makers and the media alike.

If you don't have a blog or your article is not picked up by a traditional media outlet, consider publishing your article on LinkedIn, which is one of the largest publishing platforms on the internet in terms of business-to-business (B2B) publishing, thought leadership, and other insights.

According to Devin Banerjee, a senior member of the editorial team at LinkedIn, "Consider the ABCDE best practices for publishing on our platform."

Authenticity. Represent yourself as a professional, and stay away from corporate speak or copying and pasting press release excerpts or practices such as those. Authenticity is paramount.

Bring something to the table. Advance the conversation rather than repeating what the industry conversation is already about.

Consistency is different than frequency. It might be every two weeks, it might be every month, it might be every quarter to begin with. Maybe you have a client newsletter or memo that you already work on for your company. You can post a link to that with a few lines of takeaways every quarter or every month.

Distribution. Once you publish you can tag others who you think will be interested in the topic or other experts you know of. You can tag some of your peers or others. Share the link across other social channels.

Engage. When publishing you want to prompt readers to join the conversation so they can ask you questions or make comments. Prompt them to ask you questions or to share their own take or experience with that news or trend.

THE INSTRUCTIVE TIP SHEET

The instructive tip sheet is a simple and concise list of tips or pointers that will help your audience with a specific need, task, or situation. For example:

- Four Ways to Create Stronger Content
- Five Ways to Repurpose Used Furniture
- Six Steps to Build Your Retirement Plan
- Seven Tools to Gain More Time in Your Busy Day
- Eight Ways to Get the Media to Notice You
- Nine Signs That It's Time to Change Banks
- Ten Tips for Better Communications with Clients

The ideas and topics are endless.

If you are trying to reach local consumers, you will be best served if you reach out to local media outlets.

"While it's nice for people to see you on the big TV newscast, or they see a ten-second clip of an event, [it] doesn't necessarily translate to reaching people in your audience. You're also not reaching as much of a target audience as you would be with a local newspaper or a local online news organization," said publisher and editor Tom Sofield.

"You must think, 'Do you want somebody on TV who's fifty miles away to see it, or do you want an organization that has a broad reach in your area to see it?' Which one is a better use of your time and resources?"

 On Record PR Podcast: How Businesses Can Work with LIONS— Local, Independent Online News Publishers—with Tom Sofield

If you are trying to reach corporate executives, target the print and online outlets they are most likely to read or listen to.

As with all public relations tools, have a plan and purpose for your tip sheets.
- What do you want to write about, and whom do you want to reach?
- What are the frequently asked questions?
- What does your target audience need to understand?
- How can you be more of a resource?

Once you have answered these questions, determine which outlets will be most effective.

THE WHITE PAPER

A white paper, also known as an authoritative report, is a persuasive essay that uses facts, data, and logic to illustrate a particular point. The white paper also is a way to communicate survey results and trends.

Before I dig into how you can use white papers, it is important to understand where the phrase originated. As one who is mindful of Diversity, Equity, and Inclusion (DE&I) terminology and who wants to understand the origins of language, I did my homework. According to various sources, we can blame Winston Churchill who authored the British White

Paper of June 1922. It was simply called a white paper because it was not blue. At the time most government communications were published in "blue books."

Thereafter, in government and politics, white papers were used to guide the public in making educated decisions on certain issues. However, today white papers are used more to deliver new information, survey responses, and data to a target audience. White papers also make for great in-bound marketing (which is when you share content on your website and require the visitor to provide contact information before releasing the content).

When done right, white papers have many benefits. They are as follows:

- Authoritative and persuasive and generate awareness
- Tools for in-bound marketing and lead generation
- Long-form content that can be search engine optimized
- Information that can be shared easily and distributed to your target audience
- Perceived as objective and factual with a degree of academic weight
- Credible information for media relations outreach to publish study results and other findings
- Visually appealing and have a long shelf life
- Useful to generate content for seminars, webcasts, and podcasts

White papers are rarely used by small businesses unless they are willing to invest in a third-party strategic partner. For midsize companies, if you have a marketing department or are willing to invest, white papers can be a great form of public relations and marketing. In big organizations white papers are a common practice and are usually managed by the marketing and research departments or are outsourced to a public relations or research agency.

THE BOOK

Most authors do not view writing a book as a public relations tool. However, when you author a book, you can catapult your status from an average executive to a well-known source for a particular subject.

Writing and marketing a book is a colossal task. It means dedicating an extraordinary amount of time and resources to meet your goal. There are resources available for book writing and publishing. Before you take on such a task, do your homework.

Deborah Farone, who served as the chief marketing officer of two large law firms, published *Best Practices in Law Firm Business Development and Marketing* (PLI 2019). She said, "I wrote the book with a clear purpose in mind. I wanted to use the research process as a learning exercise and a chance to try to answer the questions: What are the best practices in legal marketing, and what are law firms across the country doing that serve as markers for success?"

As a by-product, publishing the book resulted in a few unexpected immediate benefits for Deborah. She shared that several partners at law firms who read the book invited her to speak at their retreats, and several approached her with potential assignments.

"Being in marketing, I know that you generally cannot count on doing just one thing—whether the one thing is writing a book or giving a speech—to attract business. It usually takes a multiprong and cumulative approach to market professional services," she said. "The most important prong is being great at what you do."

I agree.

Well-written books serve as an added credential—validation of one's expertise and understanding of their target industry.

If you decide that authoring a book is what you want to do, Naren Aryal, CEO of Amplify Publishing Group, said, "A lot of times, people don't know how to start. What I tell them is to start with what I call a one-pager. A one-pager is simply a document that includes five or six sentences about what the book is. Just a synopsis. If you have a potential title and subtitle, great. Include it. If you've got an idea of who the target market is, great. Include it. There's no form whatsoever."

Aryal said, "Put those three or four things down on paper: synopsis, title, subtitle, and target market. Once you have that, you can share that with somebody, and that somebody can ask you questions. Then that can turn into a more robust synopsis or an outline that can turn into a table of contents that can turn into chapters. Soon you will have a book. But you must start somewhere, and the one-pager is an effective tool to get that going."

 🎙 *On Record PR Podcast: Ready to Publish a Book? Hear How from Naren Aryal of Amplify Publishing Group and Coauthor of* How to Sell a Crapload of Books

USING YOUR PUBLISHED CONTENT TO PROMOTE YOUR BUSINESS

You can use each form of writing to promote your business beyond the initial publication. The first thing to do is review the publisher's copyright guidelines. The guidelines vary.

Most publications allow you to publish reprints. In the best scenario, you can purchase a digital reprint, which you will be permitted to upload on your website and distribute as you see fit—but these rights are rare. More frequently, you will purchase printed reprints of the article, which you can then use to mail directly to your target audience.

Other ways to capitalize on your reprints:

- Add a link to the original publication on your company's website and within your online biography.
- Share the content on social media.
- Include a link to the publication in your email signature.
- Leave copies in the lobby of your office.
- Mail copies to prospective and current clients.
- Send an email to others in the industry who are good referral sources, and include a link to the publication on your website.

- Include the publication with new business materials for prospective clients.
- Share copies of the publication at programs at which you present.
- Syndicate (when permissible) your content on industry-focused websites that host articles, share readers' insights, share your content via social media, and share your content with interested readers.

Other ways to capitalize on work you have already done include:
- Writing on the same topic with a different angle or from a unique perspective
- Incorporating portions of the material into speeches or presentations
- Updating and resubmitting the piece to another publication later (depending on copyrights)

If you decide to publish thought leadership, remember that the time spent working on the material will pay off in spades.

Putting pen to paper is always a worthwhile endeavor.

LEVERAGING SPEAKING ENGAGEMENTS

A useful way to develop business for your company is to speak at business forums, industry conferences, professional association meetings, seminars, universities, and continuing education programs.

Ask yourself whether you enjoy speaking and presenting. If the answer is yes, whom do you wish to address?

Once you have answered these questions, add speaking engagements to your public relations arsenal. When you speak on a topic of interest, you are positioned as an expert in your areas of expertise. You can demonstrate your knowledge rather than sell your services or products.

WHAT TO SAY

Often executives are as stumped for a speaking topic as they are for the subject for an article. If that is the case for you, use the "FAQ Response Method," the "TOC Review Method," or the "Personal Experience Method" to determine your topic. Peruse podcasts, industry trade publications, and blogs. Use RSS feeds and Google Alerts to monitor industry news and trends. Take articles or blogs that you have written and use those same topics to create something valuable to present. For each article you write, you can create a topic to speak about and vice versa.

HOW TO IDENTIFY TOPICS

The most common dilemma is what to write about. You can come up with topics for your articles in many creative ways.

FAQ RESPONSE METHOD: One of the easiest ways to identify topics to write and speak about is what I refer to as the FAQ Response Method. Keep a notebook next to the telephone you use the most for work. Keep the pages divided by topics, such as client/customer management, industry issues, business areas, and others.

Create two columns. In the first column, write down all questions that prospective or current clients ask. In the second column, record the number of times you are asked the same question.

Once you have heard the substantive question at least three times, draft your answer or record yourself answering the question. You can use your office telephone, cell phone, voice recorder, or Zoom to capture your answer efficiently. If you are only capturing the audio recording, you will need to have it transcribed. You can use inexpensive AI transcription programs such as Temi.com or Rev.com to access a written transcript. With transcription apps, you will be one step ahead of the game when drafting written content.

TOC REVIEW METHOD: Another way to identify topics to write or speak about is to review the table of contents (TOC) of the most recent few issues of a publication that your audience reads. This is the TOC Review Method.

Ask yourself if there are any trends in these publications. What is the industry/marketplace talking about? How are themes being positioned regionally, nationally, and internationally? How can I expound on some of these issues? Are there any myths that I can debunk or inaccuracies that I can clear up? What can I say that is different, sheds light on the issues, informs the audience, and positions me as a go-to expert on the topic?

PERSONAL EXPERIENCE METHOD: Topics are determined based on one's firsthand knowledge or a great deal of research. This is the Personal Experience Method. This provides anecdotes, advice, or ideas based on your experiences using actual examples (i.e., your personal experience). This is an excellent way to educate your target audience and to share your professional prowess. This method can be used to highlight your successes.

To identify which personal experiences matter, determine what you do in your work or what products you offer that are worth sharing with others. This is the "who cares" factor. If someone will care and can benefit from your knowledge and experience, then it is worth sharing.

Do not boast or overtly promote your business or your services/products. Such behavior, whether when drafting an article or speaking at a seminar, is sales, not public relations.

GOOGLE ALERTS: Set up Google Alerts on specific issues that are garnering media attention. Consider writing about those matters and why it matters to your type of business or the industries and consumers you serve. To set up Google Alerts, you will need a Gmail account.

LINKEDIN NEWS: There's a module at the top right of your LinkedIn home feed called LinkedIn News. At any given time, there are ten to fifteen trending news items that LinkedIn editors curate. Topics are identified based on trends that the editors see, such as what people are searching for on LinkedIn and what people are talking about on LinkedIn.

 On Record PR Podcast: Leveraging LinkedIn to Develop Business, Attract Top Talent, and Become a Thought Leader with Devin Banerjee of LinkedIn

RSS FEED READER: RSS stands for "really simple syndication." RSS feed readers allow the recipient to capture and digest news, articles, blogs, and other online content. That content is plugged into a feed reader, or an interface that quickly converts the RSS text files into a stream of the latest updates from around the web. Readers usually automatically update to deliver the newest content right to your device. This approach allows you to create your own feeds filled with custom updates from the websites that are within your areas of interest or the industries you serve. There are lots of RSS apps for mobile devices. They also can be set up in Outlook, Slack, and other collaboration tools.

WHERE TO SPEAK

Not all speaking opportunities are created equal. Where you spend your time matters, and time is one resource that is not infinite.

Use the following chart to determine if a speaking engagement is worth your investment in time and resources. Think of it as a pros and cons analysis. If there are more yes answers than no answers, it is worth investing time.

	DETAILS	YES	NO

WHO ATTENDS, AND ARE THEY
A PURCHASING AUDIENCE OR A
POTENTIAL REFERRAL AUDIENCE?

CAN YOU INVITE ADDITIONAL
ATTENDEES SUCH AS COLLEAGUES,
PROSPECTS, AND/OR CLIENTS?

WILL YOUR COSTS BE COVERED,
AND IF SO, WHAT IS COVERED?

WILL YOU HAVE ACCESS TO THE
LIST OF ATTENDEES FOR YOUR
PROGRAM (BEFORE AND/OR AFTER
THE EVENT)?

HOW IS THE PROGRAM MARKETED,
AND WILL YOUR NAME AND/OR
COMPANY NAME BE INCLUDED IN
THE MARKETING MATERIALS?

WILL YOU HAVE AN OPPORTUNITY
TO INTERACT WITH THE ATTENDEES
IN ANY WAY?

IS THERE AN OPPORTUNITY TO
PROVIDE A HELPFUL HANDOUT?

CAN YOU USE THE TRANSCRIPT TO
DRAFT AND PUBLISH AN ARTICLE
AFTER THE PRESENTATION?

DOES THE EVENT INCLUDE TRAVEL,
AND IF SO, HOW MUCH TIME WILL
YOU BE OUT OF THE OFFICE?

IF THE PROGRAM INCLUDES TRAVEL,
ARE THERE CLIENTS, REFERRAL
SOURCES, OR PROSPECTS WITH
WHOM YOU CAN MEET BEFORE OR
AFTER THE PROGRAM?

WHERE TO SAY IT

Another common concern is determining where to speak for effective business development. When evaluating venues, such as for conferences and professional association events, determine whether thought leaders in the industries that you serve will be present. You may also reach other professionals in areas that complement and do not compete with yours.

INDUSTRY CONFERENCES: Industry conferences help you to reach decision makers who oversee the services. We are surrounded by countless conferences in every industry. Choose wisely. Focus on conferences that decision makers attend. When researching conferences, it might be difficult to find an all-inclusive database that is detailed and accurate. It is best to search more specifically by industry or region. Industry publications often publish lists two years in advance for the top conferences.

CLIENT AND PROSPECT SEMINARS: A seminar is akin to a lunch-and-learn during which the executive presents an important topic for a captive audience. Typical seminars often invite clients and prospects to attend, free of charge, to learn more about matters that may keep them up at night. Alternatively, business professionals may present seminars on-site at their clients' or prospects' locations. Seminars are a wise business development tool for business-to-business efforts.

COMMUNITY PROGRAMS: Community programs target general consumers and work well for professional services or products of interest to people in the community. The locations and formats for your speaking engagements are endless if you are willing to be creative. Think about the local community festival that takes place every year. Is there an opportunity to provide an ask-the-expert session? How can you participate and create value in what you share?

HOW TO SAY IT

Listening and responding is as important in a presentation as your topic choice. If you fail to deliver a dynamic presentation, you will fail to impress your audience. Remember those excruciatingly boring lectures you sat through in school? Do not be that person. Get trained to be a public speaker if you have not already. And if you are terrified of public speaking, which is quite common, then skip this tactic and focus on the things you enjoy.

If you do plan to speak publicly, identify the attendee demographics, and ask questions about who will attend and what they need from you. Then prepare your program so it is tailored to the attendees and meets their needs.

Identify specific attendees with whom you want to connect directly at the event through a scheduled one-on-one meeting. Once you know who your audience is and what its members need, determine the format and duration of your presentation. You can use PowerPoint or a lectern, flip charts, or a digital whiteboard. What matters is that you avoid relying on tools to deliver your presentation; rather, use them to enhance it.

Prepare a handout. It should have a shelf life: a checklist, an update, a list of resources. Make sure the handout is branded. Include actionable takeaways for your audience. Provide a way for attendees to follow up after the program for more information.

To support the resharing of your thoughts on social media, include the event hashtag (if there is one) and your Twitter handle name in your presentation materials.

When I speak, I include my Twitter handle, @ginarubel; the Twitter handles of my copresenters; and the relevant conference hashtag in the presentation's footer. This way people who are in attendance and on Twitter can share thought leadership, opinions, and insights with their followers and others following the hashtag.

HOW TO LEVERAGE WHAT YOU HAVE SAID FOR BUSINESS DEVELOPMENT

Once your presentation is complete, stay afterward to answer questions and to have additional conversations with attendees.

Send select attendees a thank-you letter and include additional information that may be helpful.

Follow up with those who expressed interest in learning more about you or your company or those who expressed concern about a specific matter.

Be careful not to solicit business overtly; rather, get to know how you can help those interested, and let them know how to reach you if they have a need.

I participated in a conference on crisis communications when the coronavirus pandemic began. There were more than seven hundred virtual participants, all of whom wanted to know what they should be doing to safeguard their companies, their employees, their families, and their customers.

The positive feedback prompted us to use our transcript to draft and submit an article to a trade journal on the same topic. Each of us then shared a link to the article via social media, which further capitalized on our original presentation and shared our thought leadership. Since then, the recording and the article have been shared countless times on social media.

CHAPTER 7

BUILDING A BUSINESS CASE FOR PODCASTING

By guest author Jennifer Simpson Carr

"The medium of podcasting and the personal nature of it, the relationship you build with your listeners and the relationship they have with you—they could be just sitting there, chuckling and listening...there's nothing like that."

—MARC MARON

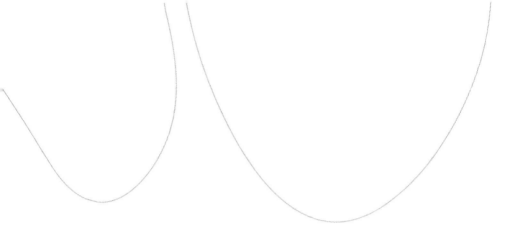

Podcasting's popularity has skyrocketed in the US, creating a means for business owners and executives to cultivate a competitive edge in their marketing efforts. There are more than 2.5 million active podcasts, comprising over sixty-two million episodes as of March 2022, and more than half of US consumers report listening to them—increasingly on their smartphones.

The average podcast listener consumes seven different shows per week and is much more active on every social media channel than non-listeners, boosting the likelihood that engagement will result in message amplification. While 81 percent of the general population is active on at least one social channel, 94 percent of podcast consumers regularly engage. And podcast listeners are educated; more than 30 percent hold advanced degrees.

C-suite executives have ranked podcasts as a preferred content source in recent surveys. As a result, podcasts are a high-engagement, low-competition way to promote thought leadership.

DECIDING WHETHER PODCASTING IS RIGHT FOR YOUR BUSINESS

Before committing to podcasting, it is essential to evaluate your organization's core values and purpose to determine how you can relate that to content. The next step is to build the business case. It is important to consider podcasting for any business, product, or service.

Key considerations to determine whether a podcast will support your business development and thought leadership include the following:

DOES IT ALIGN WITH YOUR OVERALL CONTENT MARKETING OBJECTIVES? In today's business landscape, budgets have shifted, and best-laid plans may have been thrown off track. This is a wonderful time to examine your marketing plan and reevaluate your business development goals. If you do not have a content marketing strategy or a marketing plan in place at your company, now is the time to evaluate how these new multimedia opportunities could integrate within your public relations to advance your business.

WHAT DOES YOUR COMPANY OR PRODUCT OFFER? Based on your company's offerings and individual executives' strengths, you may decide to produce a company-wide podcast that features executives from across the business or programming specific to one product or division. For division-specific podcasts, combining valuable, targeted information with engaging employee voices can then elevate and extend the company's reach through the podcast.

IS THERE A MARKET FOR YOUR CONTENT AND A VIABLE AUDIENCE? Simply stated, who cares? Think about whom you want to target, and then determine whether you can produce content that they will find useful and compelling. Think about it. Even if you are the developer of an electronic game, you could capitalize on a podcast by hosting virtual competitions with gamers and getting their tips for winning in a competitive environment.

DO YOU HAVE THE RESOURCES AND BANDWIDTH TO DEVELOP AND MAINTAIN A PODCAST? Before launch ensure that a core team of people has time and resources to dedicate to create content, as well as the budget necessary to properly promote the podcast. For this, stakeholder buy-in is essential.

DO YOU NEED TO GET CORPORATE BUY-IN? For larger companies you must determine if your company will invest in the initiative.

Some examples of podcasts that support their brands include:

- ***HBR Ideacast,*** produced by the *Harvard Business Review,* provides advice, opinion, and inspiration for professionals in any business role.
  ⚲ hbr.org/2018/01/podcast-ideacast

- ***Business of Law,*** hosted by Jason Barnwell leading conversations about corporate legal operations and the partnership with outside counsel.
  ⚲ businessoflaw.net/

- ***Freeman Means Business's Wonder Women in Business podcast,*** on which women's voices are amplified.
  ⚲ freemanmeansbusiness.com/

- ***The Heumann Perspective,*** hosted by lifelong disability rights activist Judy Heumann discussing disability culture, art, entertainment, policy, and advocacy—sure to light a rebellious fire under you to fight harder for all people.
  ⚲ judithheumann.com/heumann-perspective/

- ***The May Lee Show,*** which interviews the most impactful and relevant Asians and Asian Americans who are boldly enhancing and elevating Asian voices and issues around the world.
  ⚲ podcasts.apple.com/us/podcast/the-may-lee-show/ id1497399536

- *The Rainmaking Podcast,* hosted by Scott Love discussing client development, business development, sales, closing, prospecting, networking, negotiation, influence, motivation, and achievement.
  - *therainmakingpodcast.com*

- *The Robyn Graham Show,* hosted by Robyn Graham for entrepreneurs who want to build a strong foundation for personal brand, business, and life success.
  - *podcasts.apple.com/us/podcast/the-robyn-gra-ham-show-personal-branding-business-and/ id1491613238*

- *Tango Alpha Lima,* produced by the American Legion, on which the cohosts explore current events, interesting trends, and quirky stories of interest to the military community.
  - *tangoalphalima.fireside.fm/about*

- *Taxgirl,* hosted by Kelly Phillips Erb discussing interesting and easy-to-digest looks at tax topics.
  - *taxgirl.com/taxgirl-podcast/*

ACHIEVING BUY-IN

For larger companies, the first step to achieving buy-in is finalizing a full, go-to-market strategy before pitching the podcast initiative. This strategy should tie into the overall corporate marketing and business development plan, and it should be data driven.

Develop key performance indicators (KPIs) that track return on investment and provide case studies of companies within your industry or sector that have done it successfully.

Be prepared to communicate a draft budget that frames podcasting as a low-investment, high-value opportunity for business development to highlight your company's experience. A podcast is nothing more than an audio file that is uploaded to the internet for public consumption. Research supports using podcasts as a strategic tool to leverage your marketing and business development.

While return on investment may be difficult to quantify, the start-up investment is low. You can launch a high-quality podcast with a few hundred dollars and sustain it with a few hundred dollars a month. All that you may require at first is a microphone and some sound-editing software. With some hard work in-house or the assistance of a turnkey podcasting service, you can be up and running in less than a month.

Additionally, the costs are scalable. As you develop a following and you churn out quality content, you can increase your budget as you get more buy-in from the company. You can invest that increased budget in podcast promotion.

CURATING CONTENT THAT RESONATES

"Every episode that you produce is a business development tool and a referral opportunity, so high-quality, compelling content is the goal," said Marcie Dickson, founder and CEO of Alterity ADR.

She said, "Prospective guests on your podcast must feel good about participating, and they should feel proud to share the episode on which they are featured with their professional networks. Encourage your guests to comarket and promote their episodes through their social channels to amplify your show's reach and exposure to potential new listeners."

Engaging podcast content provides the opportunity for you to repurpose it for other marketing channels.

Publishing the show's notes on your website and on your podcast landing page benefits search engine optimization and provides additional ways for prospective listeners to find you.

By employing a "waterfall" strategy, you can transform successful episodes into blog posts, through which you can feature audiograms and short videos. Each episode's transcript is a wealth of information for developing thought leadership and marketing content.

Metrics inform your content decisions. Number of downloads is the most important metric. You may also want to track number of downloads month over month to measure growth, number of subscribers, website traffic, and relationships to referral partners. Be flexible: your KPIs may change over time, and you may find pieces of information you did not previously consider that support the podcast's continuation.

The median podcast episode duration is twenty to forty minutes, and 80 percent of listeners listen to all or most of every podcast episode they start. The sweet spot for episodes that listeners regularly complete is eight to thirty minutes.

The most successful podcasts have the following features in common:
- High-quality recording
- Engaging guests and topics
- Catchy titles that hook prospective listeners for the series and each episode
- Responsive to metrics
- Multichannel promotion

In 2020, Furia Rubel Communications launched *On Record PR* as a business development and public relations tool. While Gina F. Rubel, the author of this book, serves as the primary host discussing topics related to public relations, media relations, crisis communications, and the industries our company serves, we have also used the podcast to learn more about principal issues like DE&I and business management. Though Gina serves as the podcast's producer, all members of the team may interview thought leaders on topics of interest, and we share our expertise in several episodes each year. At the start of 2022, we recorded a podcast about trends in integrated marketing.

 On Record PR Podcast: Trends Impacting Integrated Marketing Strategy in 2022

CHAPTER 8

PRESS CONFERENCES, CORPORATE EVENTS, AND INITIATIVES

"WHATEVER YOU DO, DO IT WELL. DO IT SO WELL THAT WHEN PEOPLE SEE YOU DO IT, THEY WILL WANT TO COME BACK AND SEE YOU DO IT AGAIN, AND THEY WILL WANT TO BRING OTHERS AND SHOW THEM HOW WELL YOU DO WHAT YOU DO."

—WALT DISNEY

Public relations is the art and science of proactive advocacy by a company, individual, or brand. It requires strategic management of your position statement and key messages to reach your target audience. And through tactics such as media relations, it establishes goodwill and a mutual understanding.

You can also reach your target audience and build relationships in your community through different press events and corporate community relations programs and initiatives.

PRESS CONFERENCES

Press conferences involve someone speaking to the media at a specified time and place. The speaker controls the information they deliver, and the media is invited. There is a presumption that the speaker will answer questions posed by the media or other attendees. Press conferences should be conducted sparingly.

Hosting a press conference should be in your company's best interest when the story will excite the media. There needs to be a larger audience that will be excited by your topic. Determine if your target media outlets covered associated topics in the past and if your story has a wide consumer audience appeal. There must be a visual element to your story, a sympathetic cause, or a story that demands social justice.

As a rule of thumb, the only time a press conference makes sense is if your story warrants significant coverage and visual appeal. Otherwise, it is more efficient and less expensive to contact individual members of the media with your story than to host an event at your office or off-site location.

PREPARING FOR YOUR PRESS CONFERENCE

As with any event, go through a strategic planning process. A press conference must be well planned and strategically implemented to be successful. It is not whom you invite but when you invite them that makes a difference.

If you want to get coverage on the evening news, plan your press conference between 10 a.m. and 11 a.m. That will give the reporters and camera crews enough time to attend your program, script their voice-overs, edit the video, and have it on the production floor in time for the evening news. It is rare that your press conference will be covered live unless it is a matter that has high publicity appeal.

If you are going to host the press conference at your office, town hall, or other similar venues, determine the logistics of space and time. Consider seating, parking, security, and minimal refreshments.

If the press conference is in your office, consider the backdrop behind the speaker or signage on a podium. If there are wide-angle photographs taken, everything comes into view.

Is your company name and logo visible? Are there any distractions? If you are at the site of an incident or at a corporate location, is there a view that tells the story?

Hire a professional photographer and videographer to capture the press conference. You will have the images and footage for other use. And if all heck breaks loose in another story on the same day as your press conference, you will have B-roll to share so they may still cover your story.

B-roll is background or secondary video footage, often used as cutaway material, to provide context and visual interest to a visual story.

The following items must be addressed when planning a press conference:

- Targeted media invitation list
- Location, date, time, and duration
- Media advisory and directions
- List of speakers with printed biographies
- Press kits
- Prepared Q&A for speakers
- Media training for speakers
- Refreshments and rental needs/seating
- Sound system and podium or lectern (conduct a sound check)
- Banner/backdrop with company name and logo for photos
- Photographer
- Videographer
- Visuals
- Security (whenever necessary)
- Parking
- Follow-up

Some years ago, we helped Twilight Wish Foundation launch as a non-profit that grants wishes to seniors under the poverty level. Cass Forkin established the foundation to provide a vehicle for celebrating seniors.

When Furia Rubel was told the foundation needed help getting off the ground, the agency assisted with launch public relations and a press conference for its first granted wish. Within two weeks Twilight Wish Foundation was featured on *CNN Newsmakers* and in *Family Circle*, *USA Today*, *People* magazine, the *National Enquirer*, and *Senior Source Guide*.

The first press conference was at a cemetery on Veterans Day. Twilight Wish Foundation fulfilled the wish of Margaret Turner, who wanted to have a headstone for her deceased son, Isaiah, which their family could not afford. That November day was cold and sunny. All the major TV network affiliates, a radio news show, and the *Philadelphia Inquirer* were sending reporters. We also hired a photographer and videographer. About thirty minutes before the headstone unveiling, as we were gathered at the cemetery, we heard unrelenting sirens and watched five fire trucks pass and stop a few streets away. Unfortunately, all the TV and radio reporters went to the scene of the five-alarm fire. The *Inquirer* reporter stayed. The good news is that we had B-roll from the unveiling and were able to supply it to the news outlets that were otherwise diverted. That evening, after the hard news, every network affiliate ran the Twilight Wish Foundation story.

TOWN HALL MEETINGS

Town hall meetings are informational or discussion-focused meetings open to the public. For municipalities and other government agencies, boards of education, elected officials, and other taxpayer-funded organizations, town hall meetings are one way to communicate with both the media and the public. Town hall meetings provide attendees with the opportunity to express their opinions, ask questions, and hear from officials about specific matters of interest.

If your organization is considering hosting a town hall meeting, it is important to provide access to anyone who has interest in the subject of the meeting. Access means in-person or virtually, depending on the format you choose.

Planning a town hall meeting includes a great deal of coordination. Essential elements of your event include the location, comfort amenities such as restroom access, heating and air-conditioning, seating, security needs, audiovisual equipment, and presenters.

An example of a well-planned and implemented town hall meeting is one that Furia Rubel handled for Tinicum Township. The municipality in Delaware County, Pennsylvania, needed to address the town's residents about the status of a proposed expansion of nearby Philadelphia Airport and the lawsuit the township had filed against the airport authority.

Tinicum Township is home to about two-thirds of the Philadelphia International Airport complex. Centered on Essington, Pennsylvania, and occupying approximately five square miles, Tinicum Township faced further encroachment by the airport due to a "Capacity Enhancement Plan." This plan, which was set forth by the City of Philadelphia and the US Federal Aviation Administration (FAA), called for the acquisition of approximately 230 acres of land in Tinicum Township, part of which would be used to add a new runway near the Delaware River.

In addition to facing increased noise, engine vibration, vehicular traffic, and pollution from the airport, Tinicum Township residents stood to lose seventy-two homes, displacing approximately three hundred residents. Eighty businesses also were at risk of being displaced, impacting about thirty-three hundred employees. With these and other threats on the horizon, Tinicum Township and Delaware County filed a lawsuit seeking a declaratory judgment that would require the City of Philadelphia to gain consent from the township and the county before moving forward with the proposed land purchase.

Considering the impending lawsuit, the township named Furia Rubel its public relations agency of record. The township's goals were to increase awareness of the airport expansion plans and the dispute, increase the share of the township's voice regarding the proposed expansion, proactively communicate their messages about the potential consequences of the airport expansion, and generate positive publicity for the township regarding the dispute.

The Furia Rubel team handled strategic planning, media outreach, and community and government relations efforts, among other initiatives for Tinicum Township. One key component of the communications plan was a town hall meeting.

Furia Rubel worked with Tinicum Township leaders for weeks to plan the town hall meeting. For the location we chose a local fire hall, which had several benefits: it would be large enough to comfortably accommodate several hundred attendees; it was equipped with the necessary chairs, audiovisual capabilities, restrooms, and climate control; and the fire department was a powerful symbol of the community and carried positive connotations in the hearts of the residents.

We created the visual presentations, including custom infographics, that the township's officials would use during the meeting. These materials were clear and easy to understand, a vital component of audience comprehension. We also handled all media relations, including inviting the media to attend and coordinating their needs for coverage.

The town hall meeting was an overwhelming success. It helped the township turn the tide of the negotiations so the township and county could reach an amenable agreement that provided for the airport's expansion while minimizing the negative effects on the residents of Tinicum Township.

SIGNATURE CORPORATE EVENTS

There are many types of signature events that business-to-consumer and business-to-business companies can host. It is about identifying an offering, in-person or virtual, that speaks to your target audience to entice them to participate.

The benefits of signature events for your company can be abundant. They introduce you as an important player in the community and serve as a vehicle to connect with the public. Planning and consideration of events are the keys to making your community presence a long-term success.

Like any communication to your target audience, each event presents an opportunity for public relations. Know why you are hosting or supporting the event. Ask, "What do I want each attendee to walk away remembering about the business?" The preparation and thought you invest will undoubtedly determine whether your event is a success.

Document your plan and checklist so you create a system for duplication each year.

Make sure the time and location of your event is convenient for clients, employees, the media, and potential clients or customers (depending on whom you plan to invite). If you are hosting a special guest or dignitaries, determine their availability before you set the date.

A digital invitation is a popular and uncomplicated way to keep you and your invitees organized. If your company does not have client relationship management software in place, use digital invitation software programs, such as Evite, that help track your invitee list. Such software can be used to send reminders, updates, and to generate excitement.

Send your invitations at least six weeks before your event. Invite current clients or customers, business contacts, referral sources, colleagues, and media contacts (when relevant). Friends and family also add value to the participant list. Your guest list should include a sizable number of invitees to ensure a good turnout. Plan for less than 20 percent, which is the average response rate for most functions.

Reporters can be an essential addition to your list of invitees. Only invite a few key members of the media with whom you have existing relationships. Do not patronize them or expect news coverage. This is a relationship-building time for you and your media contacts. Make that clear.

DEFINE YOUR EVENT TAKEAWAY

Why are you inviting people to participate in your event? This is a goodwill event, so let the invitation and the event be the takeaway instead of a brochure or trinket. Make it memorable; people will participate year after year. If you spend money on promotional items, leave a lasting impact.

Determine what types of items will remain long after the event is over. What fits within the theme of your event and makes sense for you to give to attendees? There is no one single answer—it depends on your company's culture, budget, and what will hit a home run with your guests. Make sure that it is a sustainable item and does not add to the cycle of waste or increase the carbon footprint.

When the James A. Michener Art Museum, an independent, nonprofit cultural institution, was selected as the only venue in the northeastern US to exhibit Renaissance and Baroque masterpieces from the famed Uffizi Gallery in Florence, Italy, they knew that public relations was necessary. The exhibit, *Offering of the Angels: Treasures from the Uffizi*, featured works from Botticelli, Titian, Tintoretto, and other visionaries and was the first US tour of an exhibit drawn entirely from the Uffizi collection.

The museum partnered with Furia Rubel to create awareness and generate publicity surrounding *Offering of the Angels*—specifically reaching Italian and Italian American audiences. To aid the museum in achieving its goals, Furia Rubel reached out to the Consulate General of Italy in Philadelphia, coordinating a press conference at the Consul General's office. Furia Rubel also leveraged the museum's brand recognition to entice media interest while tailoring event messaging to key target audiences.

In addition to traditional press outlets, Furia Rubel piqued the interest of numerous key Italian publications, including *Italian America*, the *Italian Tribune*, *Fra Noi* magazine, *Ambassador* magazine, and numerous others.

Offering of the Angels garnered television, radio, and online coverage reaching millions of people and helping to sell out tickets.

CAUSE MARKETING, CSR, AND ESG INITIATIVES

Society expects corporations and other businesses to be socially responsible; employees demand it, and consumers expect it. There is an increased focus by businesses and their boards on cause marketing, also known as corporate social responsibility (CSR), and environmental, social, and governance (ESG) initiatives and transparency.

CAUSE MARKETING: CORPORATE SOCIAL RESPONSIBILITY (CSR)

CSR is the process of establishing a connection with the community through volunteering, charitable giving, and partnering with a cause while serving as community stewards.

There are many examples of cause marketing initiatives. You can create a meaningful grant or scholarship initiative. Host a fundraiser for an important local cause. Participate in local industry association events for their foundations. Partner with a nonprofit to volunteer time.

At the company I own, we make cause marketing a large part of our agency's experience. We offer a discounted nonprofit rate for 501(c)(3) and 501(c)(6) organizations. We provide nonprofit organizations with contractual options that allow for in-kind opportunities. We sponsor and participate in community events.

For our tenth anniversary, we spearheaded a "10 for 10" campaign, which included hosting or participating in ten cause-focused initiatives. We provided pro bono marketing and public relations services to several nonprofit organizations.

We created, launched, and participated in the Doylestown Township Adopt-a-Road Program in partnership with the township and nine other local businesses. All ten companies pledged to clean up a one-mile stretch of township-owned roadway four times a year.

We hosted a free training—Safety for Women Awareness Tactics (SWAT), featuring Vince Melchiorre, a Shotokan karate fourth-degree certified master instructor, who shared tips and tactics for women to increase their personal safety. We partnered with the local United Way Women's Initiative, promoting empowerment of women and girls.

We organized a summer food drive kickoff event for our local homeless shelter.

Our team volunteered at a Ronald McDonald House, preparing a meal for staff and guests, and we provided consulting and rebranding services to a local arm of a religious organization.

Our campaign culminated with our anniversary party hosted at a local food pantry and homeless shelter. The invitation was a brown paper bag on which we had a checklist of items needed by the pantry. We asked our guests to fill the bag to attend the event. By the time all our guests arrived, we had collected more than a ton of desperately needed food items. While serving the community, we had fun and brought attention to the shelter through the resulting media coverage.

It is imperative, however, to understand the difference between CSR and ESG.

ENVIRONMENTAL, SOCIAL, AND GOVERNANCE (ESG)

When we refer to ESG, we are not talking about charitable giving, philanthropy, volunteering, or pro bono service. In the grand scheme of ESG, those elements are minor compared to the behavior of one's company, the clients the company represents, and the people with whom the company does business. These are considered to have much greater impacts on society than individual programs.

ESG is not a small topic. I simply touch upon it in this book to bring awareness of the concept and how it plays out for businesses. ESG is a massive topic covered by many experts in books and educational programs. I am not an ESG expert; however, ESG does play a significant role in the perception and reputation of one's company. As a result, it must be addressed in this discussion related to how environmental, social, and governance considerations and initiatives affect a company's perceived character in the community.

According to Pamela Cone, social impact and sustainability sage at Amity Advisory, "ESG is environmental, social, and governance and how each company addresses those three pillars. Environment is exactly as it sounds. It is your carbon footprint and what you are doing about it. How you are making things better in the world. Social is everything that has to do with people—your own people, professional growth and development, diversity and inclusion, benefits, equal pay, other things that you do for your employees and the community." It includes corporate social responsibility and what a company is doing to make its community a better place.

Cone explained, "And then governance—the policies, practices, and procedures you have in place. Your corporate expectations. Not just of your own company's performance but the expectations on performance and behavior for your supply chain and vendors." She said, "ESG is a big, all-encompassing umbrella that covers all things to do with what a corporation's performance is in today's society."

On Record PR Podcast: What Leaders Need to Know about ESG from Leading Experts

"From a financial corporate perspective," said Pavani Thagirisa, associate GC, VP, and global head of legal for ESG at S&P Global, "it's an assessment of a company's ability to assess long-term sustainability while generating stakeholder value."

Thagirisa explains:

E: Environmental. Factors include the contribution a company or government makes to climate change, their greenhouse gas emissions, renewed efforts to combat global warming, cutting emissions, and decarbonizing to become more important.

S: Social. Human rights, diversity in the workforce, labor standards in the supply chain, any exposure to illegal labor, and more routine issues just in adherence to workplace health and safety.

G: Governance. Refers to those set[s] of rules or principles [that] we all, as lawyers, recognize. It is defining the rights and responsibilities and expectations between different stakeholders in the governance corporation. The goal of the governance pillar in ESG is to build a well-defined corporate governance system used to balance or align interests between stakeholders and work as a tool to support a company's long-term strategy.

 On Record PR Podcast: Driving Diversity, Inclusion, and Intentionality

Daniel Smallwood, the head of content for LegalESG.com and the Legal ESG Summit, adds, "The big thing right now is to define your corporate purpose. Figure out what is important to your company and its stakeholders, clients, customers, and employees. Then start addressing ESG and go from there."

He said, "There are a number of reasons why ESG matters, especially considering [current events]." At the time Smallwood was interviewed, the 2022 war in Ukraine had just broken out.

"There is a massive humanitarian crisis in central Europe that will come out of what happens. That is compounded with the number of existing issues that are going on around the world, whether it is on a global perspective or whether it is on a local perspective."

ESG is very much a part of the conversation about Ukraine, and corporations are addressing it.

Smallwood said, "When you look at the ideas that ESG is built upon, these very real-world issues, it is getting highlighted more as we move forward. If you go back, for instance, when we did not have the invasion of Ukraine, the talk around ESG was around the pandemic, the climate, and DE&I. Companies have a significant role to play in trying to address some of these issues."

The most recent war in Ukraine began on February 24, 2022. Many companies and small businesses have worked hard to identify ways to give to the people of Ukraine and the refugees. That is CSR. Many companies also decided to stop doing business in Russia and with the oligarchs. That is ESG.

These types of programs are mutually beneficial to both the community and the business. From the company's perspective, a good corporate neighbor initiative improves internal morale and assists with employee recruitment and retention. From the community's perspective, the organization's actions demonstrate the business's commitment to the public. The business generates even more goodwill when it publicizes its corporate social responsibility activities and shares them via social media, which increases brand awareness and equity.

While these initiatives and decisions can lead to positive press, the purpose should be to make a difference in the world, not to raise visibility for your business. That is integrity.

CHAPTER 9

CORPORATE AWARDS, RANKINGS, AND RECOGNITIONS

"PR IS EXTREMELY IMPORTANT, AND BEING ABLE TO USE IT IN THE RIGHT WAY MEANS EVERYTHING. YOU HAVE TO MARKET YOUR SUCCESS."

—LEE HANEY

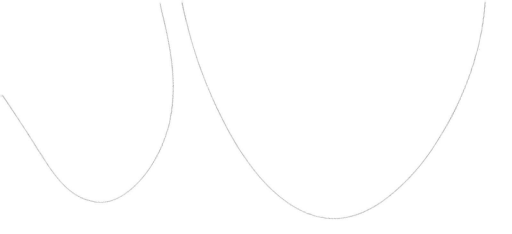

Corporate award programs can be useful public relations and business development tools. While most marketers focus on existing awards and rankings, it is possible to create branded award programs specific to your target audience.

APPLYING FOR AWARDS AND RATINGS

Your organization or executives may qualify for many awards or ratings. Look to your local business journals, chambers of commerce, trade publications, nonprofits (such as the Rotary Club and others), college alumni associations, and professional associations. Many of these outlets present a variety of awards in categories such as pro bono service, women in business, and best young leaders each year.

Trade organizations are another source of award opportunities. Examples include the American Bar Association, the National Association of Women Executives, the Association of International Certified Professional Accountants, the National Association of Realtors, the National Retail Federation, and the National Association of Women Lawyers. They all give out several recognitions each year in areas such as professional achievement, diversity, and leadership.

Business journals and other local publications present many award programs including:

- 40 under 40
- 50 over 50
- Best CEOs, CFOs, and CIOs
- Best Places to Work
- Corporate Philanthropy
- Diversity in Business
- Family Business
- Fastest-Growing Businesses

- Health Care Heroes
- Healthiest Employers
- Heavy-Hitter CRE
- Middle-Market Leaders
- Most Influential Executives
- Pride
- Top Innovators
- Women of Influence

Apply for awards that recognize community service, volunteer work, websites, corporate marketing, innovation, public relations, diversity, and anything else for which your company or its employees stand out. Set aside a budget each year for the applications, as they can be costly.

In lieu of a project management system, an uncomplicated way to track awards is to use Microsoft Excel or Google Sheets.

Include the name of the sponsoring organization and all its contact information, the early application and final application deadlines, the criteria for application, the fee, your company's submissions, and the results of your submissions.

You can then use this system to manage your award applications annually. Consider adding critical dates to your calendar, such as the early-bird deadline, the final application deadline, the announcement date, and the event date.

When your company or an employee receives an award, let others know about it:

- Write a press release for each award, and send the press release along with the headshots (with captions) to your local media, trade publications, alumni magazines, and other affinity groups with publications (print or electronic).

- Add the press release and award badges to your website.
- Post a link to the press release about the award on social media.
- Include the award information in your company newsletter.
- Include a link in your employees' email signatures to the award information on your website.
- Leave copies of your press releases in your lobby, conference rooms, and meeting areas.
- Include awards badges on your storefronts, office interiors, or leave behinds.

"It's much better to release [award] information in different ways," said David Burgess, publishing director at The Legal 500. "Create more content around social media about it. You will be surprised at how many people and your clients are looking at LinkedIn all the time, and you'll be surprised about how many people want to comment and congratulate you, which gets it higher up in visibility. All these things are simple, and any marketer worth a salt bill will tell anybody in a firm, this is how you do it. Be proud of it."

 On Record PR Podcast: The Legal 500 Publisher David Burgess Talks Law Firm Marketing, Industry Trends, and Law Firm Differentiation

To showcase recent awards and accomplishments, Furia Rubel features its recognitions on the agency's "Who We Are" page, which leads to a separate section on the website specified for awards.

CREATING AWARDS FOR YOUR TARGET AUDIENCE

The premise of a corporate awards program is to celebrate those companies and individuals who exemplify the characteristics that resonate with your organization's culture and target audience.

Awards programs should have meaning, be sustainable, and differentiate your company and its employees.

The title of the award is paramount, as it needs to reinforce your corporate brand and still be unique. When creating an award, consider your business development and public relations goals.

Ask:

- Are we trying to reach a niche industry or market segment?
- Are there any prominent figureheads in our industry or company for whom the award should be named?
- What type of award aligns with our corporate culture?
- Is there an innovation, program, or methodology that has helped people, the community, or our target industry that can be acknowledged?
- What criteria will demonstrate the characteristics of the award?
- How can the award reinforce the messages we use to differentiate our company?
- What exactly is the award? Does it have monetary value? Is it a donation to the awardees' charities of choice? Is it pro bono service for a year to a nonprofit? Is it a plaque or statue? Is it a scholarship?
- What are the promotional opportunities regarding the award?
- Will the award require an application process?
- Who will judge the applications or decide on the recipient?
- How and where will the award be presented?
- What are the marketing, business development, and public relations opportunities?
- What is the budget?

MAKING THE MOST OF YOUR AWARDS PROGRAM

Each stage of communications surrounding an award lends itself to public relations, marketing, and business development opportunities.

If an award includes a call for applications, the request should be distributed to a strategic audience including your corporate executives, referral sources, industry thought leaders, clients, and others. The request can be shared on the company's website, via email, on social media platforms, through print and digital advertising, and in various other ways.

If the judges are selected from a pool of qualified candidates internally and externally, judges' meetings are an excellent opportunity to bring people together and network.

Judging panels should include your employees, key executives within the industry, prospective clients who do not qualify for nomination, and others. After the first year, judges should include past recipients.

Once the awardees are chosen, there is an opportunity to announce the recipients in advance of a recognition event using the same communication channels that you used to announce the call for applications and again when the event is publicized.

Your prospects and clients believe in ratings, directories, and awards programs even if you do not. Take advantage of these opportunities.

INFUSING INCLUSION AND SOCIAL RESPONSIBILITY

It is important to be mindful of whom you are submitting for recognition and whom you are honoring with your corporate awards program.

Inclusivity within awards and recognitions means that the high-level people you recognize or put forward for awards reflect how you want potential clients and customers to see your company. Presenting diversity and inclusion does not mean tokenism; it means that prospects can easily identify that those members of underrepresented communities have a seat at the table and are considered a strategic part of your business.

In creating an award, there is an opportunity to create synergy with your corporate social responsibility program to give back to your community. Clients specifically look for this piece when evaluating new business partners, especially in the request for proposal or request for information response process.

CHAPTER 10

SOCIAL MEDIA ENGAGEMENT

"WE DON'T HAVE A CHOICE ON WHETHER WE DO SOCIAL
MEDIA; THE QUESTION IS HOW WELL WE DO IT."

—ERIK QUALMAN

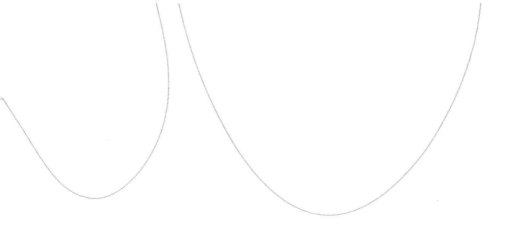

Since the early 2000s, social media engagement has grown exponentially. While social media platforms come and go, some stick, and others do not. Much like Friendster, which launched in 2002 and shut down in 2015, another platform expected to proliferate was Google+, which was a failed venture.

Do you remember Eons, Diaspora, Orkut, or Xanga? Most do not.

In 2003, MySpace was the popular social media engagement platform on which individuals set up profiles and made friends. In the same year, LinkedIn was launched for professional networking; as of 2022 LinkedIn had more than 830 million members in two hundred countries. Of those using the platform monthly, more than 30 percent access LinkedIn daily.

Facebook launched in 2004 and soon became a social media giant with more than 2.9 billion active users as of 2022.

Twitter, which launched in 2006, was inspired by the popularity of text messaging. Twitter had 326 million monthly active users worldwide as of the third quarter of 2018, 321 million as of February 2019, and 436 million as of October 2022.

For some it is hard to imagine a world without social media.

THE SOCIAL MEDIA PROFILE

Social media has changed how business professionals communicate and connect with each other and with their target audience. While not all social media platforms align with your public relations and business development strategies, they are worth exploring for growing your network of new contacts and building relationships with current and potential clients and talent.

Social media is a vehicle for thought leadership, validation (focus on your target audience), retention (post actively and frequently), and lead generation (share links to relevant content).

When was the last time you looked at the details of your social media profiles?

Review and update LinkedIn as often as possible. LinkedIn is a social media tool for professionals looking for opportunities to connect with other professionals. Make sure your profile is complete, including a full experience description in the first person and a complete work history, as well as a professional headshot. Relationships and trust are vital to landing new clients and customers, and social media is an excellent tool for establishing and maintaining relationships globally.

About 80 percent of social media business-to-business leads come from LinkedIn. The key is to establish a credible presence and create relevant and valuable content to reach your target audience effectively. Then engage with that audience through social media.

SOCIAL MEDIA ENGAGEMENT AND WHY IT MATTERS

If you are not on social media of one form or another, there are missed opportunity costs. Social media has changed the way business professionals communicate and connect with each other and with their target audience. While it remains a valuable marketing tool, social media engagement can be a challenge to navigate if not handled strategically and systematically.

Professional businesses should require all employees to use LinkedIn, at the very least, as part of their business development efforts. However, the best social media platform for you and your business depends on the audience you are trying to attract.

Organizations also should provide employees with social media training and have social media policies (this is covered in greater detail later in this chapter).

According to a 2021 Pew study of US adults, 81 percent use YouTube, 69 percent use Facebook, 40 percent use Instagram, 31 percent use Pinterest, 25 percent use Snapchat, 23 percent use Twitter, and 21 percent use TikTok.

Each social media platform has a different audience, and you need to know where your audience communicates before jumping into the fray.

You do not need to be everywhere for effective social media engagement, but you do need to understand where your audience members are, where they communicate, and the types of content that will get their attention and create conversations and engagement.

TWO TYPES OF CONTENT: CURATED AND CREATED

Much of this book focuses on content that you create, such as articles, blogs, and shareable news stories, all of which you should share on your social media networks. What about curated content?

Content curation is the process of identifying, gathering, and sharing digital content on a specific subject matter. If you are already on social media, you see curated content daily. We share links to news stories, articles, and blogs. We share quotes and images posted by others. We retweet posts of interest to our audience and ourselves.

Unlike content creation, content curation includes amassing content from a variety of *reliable* sources and sharing it strategically.

Please ensure that you and your employees verify information and content sources before sharing, as there is too much misinformation on the internet, and you do not want to create your own negative reputation for sharing false information.

LinkedIn is most popular with professionals and can be an excellent tool for engaging with businesses, current and potential clients, and recruits.

Facebook and Instagram are great for local businesses, especially those with storefronts and a local buying audience, and nonprofits.

Twitter is a great tool to use to follow and engage with the media.

YouTube is a useful tool if you have a visual story to tell. It is shareable on other platforms. Other video sharing platforms include Vimeo, Twitch, and LiveLeak.

And the list goes on.

Begin with one or two platforms. Do your research. Listen to what your customers, prospects, and colleagues are saying, and evaluate how your competitors communicate. Then continue to expand your network, participate in conversations, and showcase yourself as a thought leader in your space. Remember to connect on the platforms professionally where you know your specific audience is engaging on social media.

Set goals regarding your use of social media platforms. Always ensure that the information you share is relevant to the audience.

THE BENEFITS OF SOCIAL MEDIA MARKETING

While many executives still question social media's benefits, communicating responsibly on these platforms can transform your business.

The benefits of social media engagement for marketing, public relations, business development, and reputation management include:

- Access to marketplace insights
- Brand building, exposure, trust, and awareness
- Business development and lead generation
- Client and customer retention

- Community relationship development
- Crisis management
- Development of loyal admirers
- Differentiation
- Discovery and research
- Exposure to relevant media and engagement with them
- Growth of business partnerships and referral sources
- Increased share of voice
- Increased thought leadership, authority, influence, and exposure
- Increased traffic to the company's website, blogs, podcasts, and other online content; SEO
- Real-time communications
- Reputation management
- Transparency

It is up to you if you wish to capitalize on these benefits by engaging in social media marketing.

HOW TO MANAGE SOCIAL MEDIA ENGAGEMENT

When managing your social media profiles, use best practices.

1. **DETERMINE YOUR GOALS:** Review the organization's marketing goals, and set simple, measurable objectives. One goal may be to gain a better understanding of your target audience; another may be to learn how to use a social media platform that is new to you but interests your target audience. Ask:

   - What do you or your company want to accomplish using social media?
   - What are your/the organization's business goals, and can they be supported through social media engagement?

2. **CONDUCT A SOCIAL MEDIA AUDIT:** Determine the target audience, engaged audience, protocols, and budget needed for social media. Know your audience and who is engaging, or interacting, with the company. Research what is said about your business. An easy way to do this is to set up Google Alerts for your business, products, professionals, and clients. Also, search your organization's name on Google, Facebook, LinkedIn, Twitter, and Instagram. Ask:

- Who is the company's target audience?
- What protocols and policies are in place to manage social media engagement effectively?
- What types and sources of content are available for social media engagement (content sharing)?

One useful tool on Facebook and LinkedIn is groups. Once you join a group on social media, you can monitor conversations about your interests, industries, customers, and other relevant topics. Participate in the conversation when you have something relevant or meaningful to add.

3. **RESEARCH WHERE PEOPLE ARE TALKING ABOUT YOUR PRODUCTS OR SERVICES:** Companies may assume that LinkedIn will be the best social media platform for their targeted audience. Research products, services, and/or competitors on various social media platforms to see where your target audience is engaging the most.

4. **DEVELOP A CONTENT STRATEGY:** Make a commitment and stick with it. Create social media posts that will engage your audience and meet your social media goals. Ask:

- What types of posts will work best to meet your business's goals?

- Which social networks will work best to reach your audience?
- How and when is your audience engaging on social media?

Include the use of visual images (photos, videos, infographics) in your social media content strategy. Posts with images get exponentially more engagement.

When using images, try to use proper sizes for each social media platform. You can find image sizes cheat sheets by searching for them on the web.

Businesses can use many sources of content for social media engagement. Consider the following for content inspiration:
- Case studies
- Charity events
- FAQs and myths
- Industry news, stories, and trends
- Media coverage
- Observances (e.g., Women's History Month)
- Organization news and videos
- Seminars
- Testimonials and reviews
- Thought leadership articles, blogs, podcasts, videos, etc.
- Trending issues

You also may wish to consider sponsored content on the various social media platforms.

Sponsored content is a form of paid advertising, which allows your organization to push content to reach your target audience, not the limited number of people who see your posts organically. Sponsored content looks like editorial, and it is editorial; however, it is served to the people you want to serve.

Sponsored content should be interesting, inspiring, or educational, like any other form of written or visual content you are sharing in any medium. It can be shared in many formats, including articles, videos, images, and infographics, which typically perform well and generate engagement. Many companies sponsor content. Look at any social media platform, and you will see an overabundance of "sponsored content."

5. **IMPLEMENT MARKETING TACTICS:** Implement tactics such as creating an editorial calendar to schedule, track, and edit posts. Editorial calendar content can be scheduled in advance. Make sure that your blog posts, media mentions, press releases, events, speaking engagements, webinars, articles, and podcasts are included on your editorial calendar.

Tools such as CoSchedule, Buffer, and Hootsuite can be used to schedule social media content. There are other platforms that help you to create and share content such at Passle and others.

Remember that visuals are imperative to online success. Social media posts with images and videos get 94 percent more views than social media without visuals.

Also use hashtags (#), which allow the user to search for anything relevant to the hashtag. To find the most popular hashtags, check out hashtagify.me (although this is not a free tool).

CAUTION: Use caution when prescheduling posts for social media. Someone must be aware of what is scheduled and how it can be perceived. The last thing you want to do is congratulate a client for their work with a public entity the same day that public entity has received negative press. Being aware and monitoring your scheduled posts will help you avoid appearing tone-deaf, insensitive, or just plain ignorant to what is going on in the world.

6. **COPES—CREATE ONCE, PUBLISH ENTHUSIASTICALLY AND STRATEGICALLY:** Many digital platforms are available to help you repurpose your recently published articles, blogs, seminar content, client alerts, and other forms of useful content.

The content you create can often be shared and repurposed in multiple ways and on multiple platforms. Here are examples:

- Post a recently published article on your website as a media mention with a teaser and a link to the full story (for copyright). Then share your website's media mentions on social media platforms to help drive traffic back to your website.
- Share your media mention in an electronic newsletter or alert, driving traffic back to your website and social media platforms.
- Repurpose your content as a blog post, making sure that it is different from the published article to avoid violating copyrights, and share it on social media.
- Take the vital points from your article and write a guest post for a client or other blogs, and share those on social media.
- Create a video on the same topic as your article and upload it online. Not only do videos provide SEO value, but they also build trust and appeal to mobile users.
- Create a PowerPoint presentation using statistics, quotes, and thought leadership. Share on SlideShare for additional opportunities for engagement.
- If you have a lot of data in your presentation, create infographics. Piktochart and Canva are useful tools to help create engaging visuals for your data and talking points.
- Include a link to the article in your email signature for a few weeks: "Read my latest article in *Forbes*." Do not forget to link to your social media profiles.

- Consider hosting an online seminar that will allow you to present your topic and engage your audience in conversation, and share it via social media.
- Write an expert Q&A relating to your original article. Ask several experts to answer a question about the topic, then publish their answers as a new post, linking to your old post, sharing via social media, and tagging the experts.

Here is a visual of what content marketing and social media engagement using COPES looks like:

If you have added value to your original content, you can use these suggestions to repurpose it.

7. **GET OTHER EMPLOYEES INVOLVED IN SOCIAL MEDIA ENGAGEMENT:** One of the challenges of social media is getting employees to engage on the various social media platforms. Teach your staff how to get online, connect, share, retweet, and repost timely, relevant, and valuable content. This not only pertains to content about your company; it also should include material about employees, your customers, your industry, articles, stories by journalists that you follow, and much more.

8. **MONITOR, TRACK, AND ADJUST:** Monitor and track your social media messaging to determine whether the audience is engaging, and adjust messages and timing accordingly. Use relevant tools and apps to track engagement and refine plans based on the data results to focus on what is working best. Once you find what works best in your social media engagement, repeat it.

CORPORATE SOCIAL MEDIA ENGAGEMENT POLICIES

Businesses should develop social media policies and smart habits regarding social media engagement. Have a social media policy. Educate employees about the policies.

Elements of a social media policy include:

- **ACCEPTABLE USE:** Acceptable use policies outline a business's position on how employees are expected to represent the company on social media, restrictions on use for personal interests, and consequences for violating the policy. Acceptable use may encompass the company's purpose in establishing and maintaining social networking platforms.

- **ACCOUNT AND CONTENT MANAGEMENT:** Account management policies provide guidance on the creation, maintenance, and deletion of social media accounts.

- **EMPLOYEE ACCESS:** Employee access addresses which staff members will have access to the company's social media platforms. The policy should caution employees not to expect privacy while using the internet on any company-owned computer, cell phone, or other internet-equipped electronic devices.

- **EMPLOYEE CONDUCT:** The employment code of conduct should include three rules of engagement.

1. Your presence in social media must be transparent.

2. Protect your employer and yourself.

3. Use common sense and remember that professional, straightforward communication is best.

- **LEGAL COMPLIANCE:** Policies should include anything related to compliance in your industry. For example, if you provide health care services, you must include HIPAA regulations. If you use content or images that you do not own, always provide proper attribution.

- **SECURITY:** Companies should work with their information technology experts to ensure that the social media policy includes necessary guidelines regarding the security of data and technical infrastructure for new uses, users, and technologies related to social media. The technology concerns addressed in the policy may focus on password security, functionality, authentication of identity, and virus scans.

- **PRIVACY:** Many social media platforms allow users to set their privacy settings, which often cover areas including who viewed their profile, who can post comments and other content on the profile, and who can search for their social media page or channel. Although most of these privacy concerns apply to individual users, business users should be equally conscious.

DEBUNKING THE MYTHS OF BUSINESS SOCIAL MEDIA ENGAGEMENT

While it remains a valuable marketing tool, social media can be difficult to navigate. The new online way of interacting has changed the way businesses communicate and connect among themselves and with their target audiences. Countless myths keep executives from accepting the full value of social media engagement.

If you are not yet convinced of the importance and benefits of social media engagement, debunking these myths should do the trick.

MYTH: NO ONE TRUSTS SOCIAL MEDIA, SO WHY SHOULD I BOTHER?

There is a pervasive idea that social media doesn't work because no one trusts it, but social media can be an excellent tool for establishing and maintaining relationships. While it may not work for all businesses, it could work for yours. Research different social media platforms to find out which platforms best fit you and your target audience. Social media engagement will vary by community, industry, and sector.

MYTH: SOCIAL MEDIA IS TOO TIME-CONSUMING, HARD TO MANAGE, AND COMPLICATED.

You do not have to spend a lot of time managing your social media platforms to reap the marketing and business development benefits of listening to what contacts are saying. It also helps to stay up on the latest trends. All social media engagement is based on the core principles of informing, educating, and entertaining audiences. Valued content on the right platform is a universal requirement if you want to make the best use of your social media engagement.

MYTH: SOCIAL MEDIA METRICS ARE MEANINGLESS AND HARD TO TRACK OR MEASURE.

Social media is a platform to build your company's brand, promote the great work of your employees, and promote your products or services. Each platform has various tools built in for tracking impressions, click rates, engagement, and demographics. There also are third-party tools like Google Analytics that make it easier to track your website's traffic, visitors, page views, and referrals. WordPress also has an analytics tool to help you track and measure data. Hootsuite and HubSpot have reports on metrics and trends that provide a holistic analysis on what is happening to your content's and website's performance, email campaigns, lead nurturing, and contacts in sales funnels to help you measure data.

If someone is engaging with you on social media, you can assume the person is interested in your products or services.

MYTH: SOCIAL MEDIA IS ONLY A PLACE TO PUSH OUT CONTENT.

When tracked and measured, it is possible to show real return on investment to prove you are getting business from your work. Monitor and listen to see what your clients are doing and saying.

Furia Rubel client Willig, Williams & Davidson, which is a union law firm in Philadelphia, created a social media committee. Members draft new and timely content, share relevant news stories, and engage on hot-button issues on their Facebook page. When the firm shared a Supreme Court decision that affected one union, it garnered 6,636 views, thirty-six shares, and more than thirty positive comments within hours. In addition, Bloomberg Law interviewed Lauren Hoye, one of the firm's labor attorneys, because of a Google search that brought up a relevant blog she published and shared via social media.

MYTH: SOCIAL MEDIA DOES NOT AFFECT THE BOTTOM LINE OR BRING IN BUSINESS.

You cannot always show an ROI on social media engagement. Have a strategy that is aligned with your goals and includes talking to the right audience in the right places. Use Google Analytics to show trends and validate that prospective buyers are going to your website through social media.

THE FUTURE OF SOCIAL MEDIA ENGAGEMENT

No one knows what is in store for social media or what the next best social media platform will be. What we know for now is that social media is here and likely to stay—while it will continue to evolve.

With the constant changes in technology, it will be interesting to see how social media continues to change our daily work and personal lives.

For now, smart executives and marketing-savvy businesses are strategic and systematic with their relevant and timely social media engagement.

CHAPTER 11

INTERNAL COMMUNICATIONS

"THE DIFFERENCE BETWEEN THE RIGHT WORD AND THE
ALMOST RIGHT WORD IS THE DIFFERENCE BETWEEN LIGHTNING
AND A LIGHTNING BUG."

—MARK TWAIN

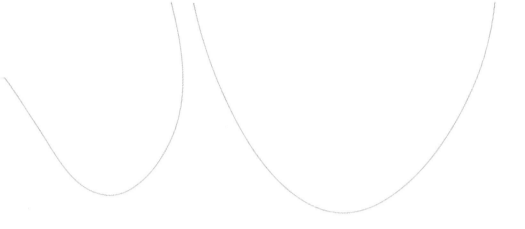

The strategies and tactics of public relations and marketing often are focused on external audiences. That is why much of this book is dedicated to topics like media relations, thought leadership, and other forms of content and information that reach outside the business. Internal communications always have been important and an integral part of a company's communications efforts.

A study by Axios HQ, an internal communications platform, revealed alarming findings. In a survey of more than four hundred employees, communicators, and executives from various industries and company sizes revealed a deep chasm between corporate communicators and their internal audience.

Seventy-four percent of communicators think they write concise and effective messages, while 60 percent of employees disagree. Forty-five percent of public relations professionals say they do not receive enough feedback from their communications, while 31 percent of employees say they lack a proper feedback channel. Fifty-nine percent of communicators say the most challenging part about internal communication is getting employees to read it. Forty-seven percent of communicators say their organizations measure the effectiveness of internal communication.

The survey results suggest that ineffective communication can create "underproductive and disengaged employees" as "cross-organizational updates" are "unclear, inconsistent, and weak." And when employee engagement wanes, trust follows close behind.

GOALS OF EFFECTIVE INTERNAL COMMUNICATIONS

I recently met Neil Tunnah, founder and owner of The Performance Chain, headquartered in Australia. It is an international company that works with business owners, managers, and teams to design and implement the processes and systems that optimize individual, group, and team performance, ultimately delivering high performance in the workplace.

Neil also is a high-performance rugby coach who coaches D1 15s men's rugby at Mount St. Mary's University in Emmitsburg, Maryland. He has more than twenty years of experience helping individuals, teams, and organizations optimize performance and achieve success.

Neil focuses on "a framework of building robust long-term relationships, world-class communication, attention to detail, and the ability to reflect, review, and improve in environments where individuals are inspired to thrive." He said, "This is what a team is all about." And this is exactly why internal communications are so important.

When Neil and I spoke, we talked a great deal about how a strong leader or leadership team must structure culture, leadership, and performance to set and achieve goals. This means creating a sturdy foundation for internal communications and understanding what those communications must accomplish.

Neil said, "As leaders, to achieve high performance, we must nurture an environment where everyone has the confidence to share thoughts, ideas, and feedback. Honesty is critical for growth, development, and performance. For true honesty to be achievable, we must connect our teams on a deeper level, a level where there is an emotional connection to each other and the common goal or business objectives. When people care deeply about the purpose, objectives, and values because they have been connected to their own intrinsic motivators, then teams can truly achieve high performance."

The bottom line is that it comes down to authentic, empathetic, and effective internal communications.

Your internal communication goals should include:

- Fostering a culture where employees are comfortable speaking to management and to one another
- Providing a forum for open and direct dialogue
- Differentiating how and when to communicate messages internally for everyday situations versus more challenging issues like leadership changes, civil unrest in the community, mergers and acquisitions, decreased revenues, and local, regional, or international crises
- Deciding how and when to communicate to diminish internal fear, rumors, and media leaks
- Incorporating unifying language that recognizes diversity, supports inclusion, and promotes a sense of belonging among all
- Adopting tools and technologies that reach a remote team and suit varied learning and attention styles
- Creating internal processes to establish and preserve best practices

The Axios HQ study also identifies what employees seek from workplace communication:

- Shorter, multi-item updates that are relevant to their roles
- Clearer, more transparent updates to cut out surprises
- In-person opportunities to discuss important updates
- Ways to share their voice and offer feedback

HOW TO CRAFT INTERNAL COMMUNICATIONS

Internal communications must speak to everyone on the team. To do so, after you have crafted a message, ask yourself the following questions.

- What is the most effective manner with which to communicate the message?
- Does this message have authenticity and transparency?
- Does this message have all the context it needs to make sense to everyone on the team?

- Can this message resonate with everyone at every level in our company (emotional intelligence)?
- Does the message use inclusive language?
- Does the message take into consideration cultural or regional differences? For instance, if you have offices in the US and UK, you may want to use both terms for the same item when the words ("car park" / "parking lot") or spellings ("colour"/ "color") differ.

TOOLS FOR INTERNAL COMMUNICATIONS

The most frequent concerns we hear from clients during our communication assessments are that the organization lacks effective internal communications or that the company is not transparent. Often management fails to share goings-on with employees, contributing to frustration and resentment and resulting in a wide variety of missed opportunities to grow and improve the business.

In addition to simply meeting with members of your team and sharing information with them, thankfully, there are many tools for effective internal communications.

DAILY MEETUPS: If possible, daily or regularly scheduled briefings are helpful to maintain a team environment while openly communicating with staff. For small businesses, daily or morning meetups are an option.

Years ago at Furia Rubel, we implemented "daily stand-up" meetings where we would all stop what we were doing and gather in the center of the office to reconnect and refocus. They began as two per day, one at 9 a.m. and the other at 4 p.m. Over time our daily stand-ups changed. Rather than the whole office meeting in the morning, only those who needed to check in with one another did so. In the afternoon, a reminder popped up at 4 p.m. for the entire available staff to meet. When the company went virtual, we continued the tradition as a "Morning Teams Meeting," which we currently host three days a week. In February 2022 I added a weekly

"Open Office Hour" via Zoom so any member of the team could quickly visit, ask questions, or simply talk about the issues of the day.

What I like about morning meetups is that they allow members of the team to connect with one another and highlight the most pressing and important issues of the day. It also helps teammates to know what is going on with one another, clients/customers, strategic partners, and the like. It also helps to foster a culture of inclusion. Occasionally, I will also call for an icebreaker so we can all get to know one another better since our team members are in several states.

REAL-TIME CHAT TOOLS: I admit, when a member of our team first introduced Slack to our agency in 2010, I was against implementing yet another form of communication. At that time, I was getting too many emails and texts to think about adding another channel or responsibility. When I am wrong, however, I admit it. And I was wrong. Slack has increased our productivity greatly.

Our team uses Slack for all internal communications and questions, cutting down our use of emails by more than 30 percent. In addition, everyone in each channel can see the dialogue, and the communications are saved in each channel, making it easy to recall information.

Should you consider a real-time chat tool, here are some options.

- Chanty
- Cisco Jabber
- Discord
- Flock
- Flowdock
- Google Chat
- Mattermost
- Microsoft Teams
- RingCentral
- Rocket.Chat
- Ryver
- Slack
- Yammer

INTRANETS: An intranet is a local or restricted computer network used for sharing communication with a specific audience. Usually, a company's intranet is used so employees can securely share information, communicate more efficiently, and collaborate. An intranet provides a central repository for information and company data. It usually allows for personalization of the content, and many have social elements similar to social media but within a private platform.

Many intranets also include to-do lists, employee directories, employee birthdays and anniversaries, news about employees and their families, and much more.

TIPS FOR DELIVERING EFFECTIVE INTERNAL MESSAGES

In addition to ensuring that each communication is inclusive and effective and reaches its intended audience, here are additional tips to help you meet your internal communication goals.

CHOOSE YOUR WORDS WISELY: All words matter. There is a significant difference between "yes, and" and "yes, but." As you choose your words, think about the tone and what can be taken out of context or where people might read into the meaning.

Siri Lindley, a two-time world champion triathlete and triathlon coach, said, "Your experience of any situation can be completely changed by the words that you use. I don't know if you know of anyone in your life that had one bad thing happen and you say, 'Well, how was your day?' 'Oh, it was a horrible day. This one thing happened.' Now using the word 'horrible' makes that one thing that happen[ed] so much worse than it probably was, instead using language of, 'I experienced something difficult.' When I got leukemia, I was told I had a 5 percent chance maybe of surviving, but there was no way. I said, 'OK, this is an opportunity. This is an opportunity for me to grow and to learn and to realize that there is something that I am meant to learn through this process.' A problem is more an opportunity. It's an opportunity to grow."

Lindley said, "Another example is the word 'failure.' When we think that we have failed, it's a horrible feeling, and that can demoralize you, and that can keep you from trying again or taking on big things again. I changed the definition of failure to 'learning.' Failure is learning. When I fail, I learn. When I learn, I grow. When I grow, I make progress."

 On Record PR Podcast: Living Fearlessly Authentic with Two-Time World Champion Triathlete Siri Lindley

BE CONSISTENT WITH YOUR MESSAGES: Messages come in the forms of written words, body language, and the actions we take. If you are trying to communicate internally that everyone is going to make it through a particularly challenging time, be sure that you are consistent. If the messages are delivered in person, via recording, or virtually via a video platform, your facial expressions and body language must comport with the message. We all know that actions speak louder than words, so don't say one thing and do another. That is the quickest way to lose trust and eventually your team.

COMMUNICATE REGULARLY: Internal communications must happen consistently, and this does not mean you must have all-hands-on-deck meetings all the time. It might simply mean a monthly email from the person in charge checking in with the entire team. It could mean quarterly updates from division leaders, and it could mean an annual meeting where everyone is brought up to speed about the company. No matter how often you communicate, consistency is key.

PRIORITIZE INFORMATION: The simple truth is that most people have an attention span shorter than that of a goldfish. If that is the case, put your most important messages first. It is as simple as that.

BE CONVERSATIONAL AND AVOID JARGON: Remember that you are communicating with people. Even if you are sending an email, it need not be overly formal. Use a conversational tone. Be authentic. Avoid jargon.

PACKAGE INFORMATION IN CATEGORIES: Use headers or boldface type to separate ideas. Just as I am doing in this book by bolding specific statements before adding more information, you should do the same in your internal communications.

BE REPETITIVE: Remember that no one reads everything the first time they see it. Sometimes you need to distribute messages via various channels.

EXAMPLES OF INTERNAL MESSAGES

CYBERSECURITY UPDATE

When two employees messaged me with screenshots of what appeared to be phishing scam texts, I investigated further. I learned that they had been hit with the "boss scam." Since they were likely not the only two to get hit with it, I drafted and sent the following missive via our instant message tool, Slack. I also sent it via email if anyone missed it in Slack.

> **THE BOSS SCAM:** If you get a text message that appears to come from me that says something like, "I am in a meeting and I need you to do something urgently," do not respond. It is the boss scam (more about it below).

> **IF YOU HAVE RECEIVED OR DO RECEIVE A SUSPICIOUS MESSAGE,** here is where you can find information on how to block the number and report it as junk.
> - Apple: support.apple.com/en-us/HT201229
> - Android: support.google.com/messages/answer/9061432?hl=en

Boss scams target employees working remotely with texts and emails from fraudsters posing as employers and usually lead to the employee being asked to purchase a gift card. This scam has been on the rise. Two of our employees received fake texts supposedly from me yesterday. The good news is that we conduct ongoing cybersecurity training, and they knew to alert me first.

OTHER THINGS YOU SHOULD KNOW: When you look at the message (at least on the iPhone), it color-codes the message so you can determine if it is an SMS (standard text message) or a messaging service like Apple's iMessage. If the message is in fact a text message, you will need to reach out to your wireless carrier to report the messages. If the message is an iMessage (or another messaging service), you will need to contact the host of that service, such as Apple for iMessage. In addition, depending on how the messaging service is configured on your phone, it could also be an email provider that is the source of the message, in which case you may need to report the abuse to the email provider.

INTENDED MERGER

From the CEO:

I am excited to tell you that the boards of directors of Company A and Company B agreed to combine to form a new bank. Our new, unified bank will have XX branches with no overlap of branch offices and will hold $X.X billion in assets. There will be no layoffs.

Together we will have the resources and the scale to help our communities grow and prosper. We will provide the same personalized attention to customers, in the same locations, and with added strength and an increased profile.

The new, unified bank will have a new name, which will distinguish it from other banks operating in our communities, and will deliver a consistent message throughout our markets. We expect to unveil the new identity by XXXX.

We now begin the process of obtaining regulatory approval for the unification, after which the new bank officially will take shape. We will update you regularly on the progress of plans to integrate both organizations and the timeline.

A press release will be sent shortly to the news media to announce our exciting plans; a copy will be placed on our website. Later today members of senior management will be visiting your locations to discuss this announcement further.

I am confident each of you will continue to improve the financial lives of our customers, as we have done for many years. Thank you for all you do today and for what you will do tomorrow.

MANAGEMENT NEW YEAR MESSAGE

From the CEO:

As we settle into the rhythm of a new year, I wanted to take a few minutes to reflect on the developments of this year and look ahead to what next year has in store.

As we continue to attract work from innovative clients shaping the national and global economy, we must continue to provide best-in-class services. During the last twelve months, our successes include:

- Success
- Success
- Success

This excellent performance is the result of the outstanding work that every team member offers. Thanks to each of you for your contributions.

As we look forward to next year, we have the right people on our team and the right practices in place to continue our success in the new year.

I am grateful to work with colleagues of such integrity and quality, who provide our clients with consistently excellent service. As the new year begins, we have much to be excited about.

Happy New Year!

BUILDING DIVERSITY, EQUITY, INCLUSION, AND BELONGING INTO YOUR INTERNAL CULTURE AND COMMUNICATIONS

In our podcast *On Record PR*, we often ask guests questions about internal communications with a focus on diversity, equity, inclusion, and creating a sense of belonging. We have received wonderful insights from our guests.

Furia Rubel's director of strategic development, Jennifer Simpson Carr, asked WNBA legend, vocalist, actor, model, and spokesperson Kym Hampton what leaders can do to provide the resources and opportunities for retaining diverse talent who have longevity and fulfilling careers within an organization. Kym said:

People will want to stay when they have coaches and teachers who pour into them. Richard Branson said, "You want to train people well enough so they can leave. But you want to treat people well enough that they don't want to." It is a quote that basically says you prepared me to go out and have a successful life, but I find that I want to stay because I want to be around the positivity.

Leaders of companies must be so involved and good with the people that work for them, so they want to stay. It must start at the top.

It's kind of like building an NBA team, or building any type of team, but we'll say an NBA team where you have your star player. In one company the star player might be a white kid, for example, but you must start building a team around him. And it should be a diverse team. You can't have only one person that can shoot. You need to have people that can play defense. You need people who are great communicators on the court. You need quick people. You need so much to build a championship team. That's when they think about their companies. They must think along the [lines] of, "What do I need?"

Make sure you recruit the best—not because of what their skin looks like, but because they are the best.

 On Record PR Podcast: A Winning Game Plan for Recruiting and Retaining Diverse Talent with Kym Hampton

UNDERSTANDING AND ELIMINATING MICROAGGRESSIONS

Today's definition of microaggression is credited to Derald Wing Sue, a professor of counseling psychology at Columbia University. Since 2007 he has authored several books on microaggressions, including *Microaggressions in Everyday Life: Race, Gender, and Sexual Orientation.*

Derald says that microaggressions are the everyday slights, indignities, put-downs, and insults that members of marginalized groups experience in their day-to-day interactions with individuals who are often unaware that they have engaged in an offensive or demeaning way.

Microaggression is a term used to describe casual, daily types of comments or statements that intentionally or unintentionally reflect implicit biases against specific groups.

Microaggressions may seem innocent or harmless, but they impact the receiver or groups of receivers negatively.

Microaggressions are the lived experiences of a group of people—the daily, small bits of drama that take place overtly or inadvertently.

Microaggressions reflect beliefs that have been so engrained in us that we often do not recognize the impact of the behavior on others. Whether done innocently or out of willful ignorance, the behavior is harmful nonetheless.

Microaggressions cause systematic, sustained trauma.

Microaggressions happen all day, every day, everywhere, and in every context.

EXAMPLES OF MICROAGGRESSIONS

Offensive to people of Asian descent:

- Saying "open the kimono"
- Referring to all Asians as being smart
- Referring to Asians as Orientals
- Referring to COVID-19 as the Kung Flu, China virus, Chinese virus, or Wuhan virus

Statements offensive to Black and brown people:

- You speak so well. You don't sound Black.
- You're the first Black person I have known who [insert anything here].
- Race isn't an issue.
- I don't see color.
- There is only one race, the human race.
- You don't sound urban.
- How often do you wash your hair?
- Are you wearing your hair like that for work?

Statements offensive to people with disabilities:

- Can I pray for you?
- Have you tried X [to solve a disability]?
- Don't you miss X [something one assumes you may have been able to do previously]?
- Disability isn't part of diversity.
- Great job [in a patronizing tone].
- You're so brave.

Statements offensive to immigrants and people with accents:

- Your English is flawless.
- Where are you from?
- Where are your people from?
- Where were you born?
- Where is your country?
- How long have you been in America?
- How did you get here [referring to America]?
- Is your family in America too?
- Do you go back to your country?

Statements offensive to Jewish people:
- Telling people they should get a Jewish lawyer
- Referring to someone as a JAP or Jewish mother
- Stating that one is not anti-Semitic because they have Jewish friends
- Use of the terms "Jewing," "Jewing down," or "Jewed down"

Statements offensive to LGBTQIA+ individuals:
- Stating that the use of personal pronouns is silly
- Stating that there are only males and females
- Stating that marriage is only valid between a man and a woman
- Saying "it's so gay that [insert anything here]"
- Using the phrases "just us girls" or "just us guys"

Statements offensive to older individuals:
- You are so cute.
- Are you sure you should be doing that?
- I would never have guessed you're that old.

Statements offensive to women:
- Do you work?
- Are you a stay-at-home mom?
- Are you a nurse or schoolteacher?
- Oh, you must be Mrs. [man's last name].
- I didn't know girls [played rugby, wrestled, played football, played hockey...].
- Girls aren't good at [insert anything here].
- Are you his assistant?
- Who wears the pants in the house?
- Women should be barefoot and pregnant.
- There's no place for women in [insert anything here].

Statements offensive to one who wears traditional, cultural, or religious garments such as a kente, sari, kimono, hijab, turban, kippah, or burqa:

- Why do you wear that?
- Isn't that uncomfortable?
- Why are your clothes so bright [or dark]?
- You're always dressed like you're going to a funeral.

I'd be remiss if I didn't share some of the microaggressions that I've experienced as an Italian American, even though I am a white woman who was born in the United States. These are some that I recall.

- You're Italian. You have child-bearing hips.
- What do you mean you never watched *The Sopranos*? I thought you'd love it, being Italian.
- Do you know John Gotti, boom boom? [asked of me when I was visiting Paris at age twenty-seven]
- You must love to eat pasta.
- *The Godfather* must be your favorite movie.
- How many people in your family are named Vinny?
- That's such a Guido thing to do [said in general, not referring to my grandfather].

In an article in *CBE: Life Sciences Education* (published by the American Society for Cell Biology) entitled "Language Matters: Considering Microaggressions in Science," Collin Harrison and Kimberly D. Tanner said it best:

Language matters. What we say can have profound effects on an individual's sense of belonging, self-efficacy, and science identity. …We can ourselves use language that may slight or invalidate someone else, even with only the best of intentions. We all make mistakes and may lack awareness of the way our words may affect those around us. We also all have unconscious biases that influence how we interact with one another. While we may or may not be aware of, or effectively address, biases, they are a part of everyday life for nearly all humans.

ACTIONABLE STEPS COMPANIES CAN TAKE TO BE ALLIES TO DIVERSE COMMUNITIES

GET INFORMED: To communicate internally (or externally), you need to have a better understanding of your audience. That means understanding who they are and where they're coming from. This does not mean making assumptions; it means learning about people, diverse communities, and the issues that you might not have experience with.

Nydia Han, 6ABC Action News coanchor, investigative reporter, and AAPI journalist, said, "Unfamiliarity drives fear; fear drives hate. If people take the time and initiative to learn about other people, learn about other experiences, that is absolutely the first step. Follow people who do not look like you on social media. Follow people who have a dissimilar experience and a different perspective so that you can understand, and you'll be alerted and informed as you go through your social media accounts. The first step—acknowledgment and understanding."

 🎙 *On Record PR Podcast: Talking Diversity with 6ABC Action News Coanchor, Investigative Reporter, and AAPI Journalist Nydia Han*

CREATE CHANGE WITHIN YOURSELF: This is where Kym Hampton believes we must start. She said, "It starts with each company leader out there, in every industry, and then it trickles down. Everyone must be willing to have a different viewpoint, to be open, and to learn. A lot of people are so out of touch. They don't know what goes on. It's about putting yourself in the shoes of other people."

LEAD INCLUSIVELY: Nydia Han said, "There are times when maybe there's a person of color in the room who isn't quickly speaking up. Think about and understand it may not be because that person doesn't have an opinion or doesn't have something to say or doesn't have information, but maybe this is not an environment in which that person feels comfortable to speak up. Maybe you need to ask or call on that person or do it outside of the meeting. There are a lot of ways people can consider and meet their employees where they are."

MAKE BELONGING THE GOAL: Reggie Shuford, the executive director of the American Civil Liberties Union (ACLU) of Pennsylvania, said, "Diversity isn't enough. Inclusion isn't enough. Our aspirations must be more. When I am thinking about workplaces and the communities that we want to create and the world that we want to live in, the goal is belonging. Everybody, particularly given the amount of time people spend at work, wants to feel like they belong. Like they truly belong—like they are an integral part of the enterprise. Their work is valued. They are valued. They feel safe. They feel secure. They feel they matter; their opinions matter. Their opinions are solicited. Their opinions help inform the way the work gets done. To me that's what belonging is. Authentic belonging, inclusion, diversity, and equity (ABIDE) is my way of putting it all together."

 On Record PR Podcast: Belonging Is the Key to DE&I Efforts: An Interview with Reggie Shuford, Executive Director of the ACLU-PA

CHAPTER 12

HOW TO MEASURE PUBLIC RELATIONS

"YOU CAN'T IMPROVE WHAT YOU DON'T MEASURE."

—PETER F. DRUCKER

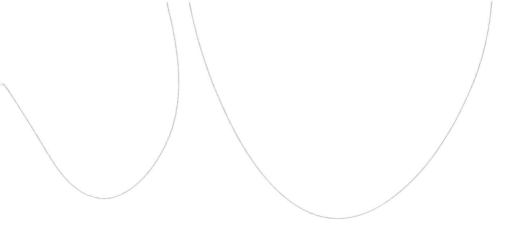

The Chartered Institute of Public Relations (CIPR), the European equivalent to the Public Relations Society of America (PRSA), said, "Public relations is about reputation—the result of what you do, what you say, and what others say about you. It is the discipline, which looks after reputation, with the aim of earning understanding and support and influencing opinion and behavior. It is the planned and sustained effort to establish and maintain goodwill and mutual understanding between an organization and its publics."

The essential language in CIPR's definition is that PR is about "the results of what you do, what you say, and what others say about you." So why measure results?

A 2021 Muck Rack PR metrics survey of five-hundred-plus public relations professionals was meant to determine which metrics mattered most to them and how they will approach measurement and reporting in 2022.

More PR pros will focus on social media in 2022: 60 percent will measure social shares and social engagement. Ninety-four percent agree that placements were a top priority in 2021—and that will remain unchanged in 2022. Twenty-eight percent plan to report on consumer sentiment in 2022, a 10 percent increase over 2021.

Throughout this book I have talked about the intersections among marketing, public relations, and business development and how public relations must support the overall business goals of the organization. By measuring your PR efforts, you will:

- Gain insights to aid future investments and decision-making
- Get a clearer picture of how your business is perceived
- Prove the value of your PR campaigns
- Identify which tactics are working and which are not
- Refine your campaigns to improve outcomes
- Evaluate performance to plan successful future PR strategies, set your budget, and refine your KPIs

Chapter 2 explains the steps in public relations planning. The last step calls for measuring public relations outcomes because, as I said earlier:

If you do not measure the effect of your public relations, you are only half communicating. You created a solid public relations plan, targeted your audience, identified your positions, crafted your messages, laid out your calls to action, and implemented an extensive list of tactics. But you are only three-fourths of the way there. To complete the process, you must measure the results. Without measuring results, you are wasting the money you spent on creating and implementing your plan.

During the planning phase, you would have defined the S.M.A.R.T. goals and the measurement metrics you plan to use. The metrics must support your overall business goals, and your goals define which metrics you use. Pay attention to coverage, exposure, reach, placement, demand, impact, calls, leads generated, and new business (i.e., conversions).

Ask the following questions:

- What were the goals, and have we achieved them?
- What has happened because of our PR efforts?

- How are we tracking the success of our PR efforts?
- How can we improve our PR efforts?

Public relations measurement and evaluation are essential to determining the effectiveness or value of a strategic plan or effort. It remains one of the most discussed, evolving, and challenging issues in the industry.

In the short term, public relations measurement and evaluation involve assessing the success or failure of programs, strategies, activities, or tactics by measuring the outputs, outtakes, and outcomes against a predetermined set of objectives.

In the long term, public relations measurement and evaluation involve assessing the success or failure of much broader efforts that were formulated to improve and enhance the relationships that professionals and their businesses maintain with key constituents.

There is no all-encompassing research tool or technique that will measure and evaluate public relations effectiveness. Measuring media content, for example, can provide insight into how much exposure your messages received, but it cannot, by itself, measure whether your target audience responded to the messages or if your company has grown as a result.

With all of this in mind, reconsider the public relations objectives listed in chapter 2.

Increase awareness about your company and its products or services. Build name recognition of your organization, its executives, and its products or services. Announce a merger, acquisition, or office relocation to facilitate easy communication between your company and its clients or customers. Increase new business and profits. Retain or grow existing client accounts. Acquire prospective clients in a new market segment. Create demand and interest from prospective employees. Develop employee goodwill. Garner media attention regarding a successful business venture, product development, charitable initiative, or expansion. Generate referrals from thought leaders. Manage your company's (or your personal) reputation.

How can you determine whether you have met these objectives?

TRACK NEW BUSINESS TO ITS ORIGINS

With the pressure to be competitive and retain and win more customers, businesses know they must thoroughly implement their communications plans. But many small and midsize companies do not take the time to learn where their business originates.

How do you know for certain that 35 percent of your new cases came from referrals or that the event your organization hosted did not result in any new clients? If you do not ask where each lead comes from (its origin), you are only doing half the job.

OUTPUTS, OUTTAKES, AND OUTCOMES

- **OUTPUTS:** The most basic form of measurement, outputs measure what we produced and how we did in producing it. Was it on time? On budget? On message? For public relations this often means measuring the number of media placements, which is only a starting point.

- **OUTTAKES:** Outtakes focus on who was reached instead of what was produced. How many people read the article? Who downloaded the white paper? How many media outlets showed up for the press conference? How many new contacts registered for the event? How much traffic was there to the website as a result?

- **OUTCOMES:** The most challenging and essential form of measurement, outcomes look at changed behaviors attributable to your efforts. Who called the office for more information? Who became a client? Who referred new business? Which clients increased their business? Did you generate more qualified leads year over year?

There are two types of causation: actual cause and proximate cause. Actual cause (i.e., cause in fact) is determined by the but-for test.

But for the action, the result would not have happened. Stated more simply, "But for the [insert PR tactic here], ABC client would not have known about our company offerings."

Proximate cause is an action that produced foreseeable consequences without other intervention.

With public relations, to determine how a prospect became a client or customer requires several foundational elements and best practices. Otherwise, it is almost always a guessing game.

Consider what happens when a prospect calls a service provider. Here are a few of the scenarios:

1. General consumer client is looking for a contractor. She heard about your company and calls the main number. Then what? How is the call handled? What questions are asked? How is the call directed?

2. General consumer client from scenario 1 (above) calls the company's main number but knows she wants to speak with Melody Henderson because she was listed on the website as the company's president of residential real estate contracting. What happens next? What questions are asked? How is the call directed?

3. A nonprofit was referred to your association management company to discuss whether the organization would like to participate in a request for proposal. The executive director does not remember the name of the person to whom she should talk. What happens next? What questions are asked? How is the call directed?

In scenarios 1 and 3, someone must decide who will get the call. However, has the company provided them with the requisite training to ask certain foundational questions and to capture the answers? Or has the organization left all information-gathering responsibilities to the support staff?

In scenario 2, it is up to the specific professional to document how the prospective client came to the organization and should have protocol for the next steps. What processes do you have in place to ensure that the individual captures all the right information—not only the client's origination?

What about the prospective leads who call and do not convert into new business? How does the company track those opportunities and from whence they originated?

What if your receptionist asked how the caller heard about your company and recorded the response in a database or the company's client relationship management system (detailed more fully later in this chapter)? What if you found out that your organization received ten calls from your most recent seminar, but none were converted to a client? Then you could reevaluate your efforts. Instead of asking why your seminar did not generate leads, you would focus on why those ten prospects did not convert to clients. Did you target the right people? If so, was there a failure somewhere between intake and closing the deal with the potential clients? And do you have systems in place to follow up with the leads to find out?

In the same situation, let's suppose that plenty of people attended your seminar, but no prospects called your company afterward. If your audience was well-defined and your messages were on target, why did the seminar fail to make an impact? Did you ask attendees to review the seminar? If so, the answer may lie in their evaluations. If not, put your evaluation, tracking, and measurement programs in place to determine the value of your programs. If your seminars do not result in leads, maybe seminars are not the best way to reach your target after all—or the topic covered may not be the best for your audience.

I spent more than a year speaking at national conferences on social media engagement for professionals. The programs were heavily attended; the evaluations were stellar. Attendees loved the content and asked tons of questions. The phone never rang. Not a single prospect called to ask how our company could support their social media efforts. What I finally determined is that it had nothing to do with the topic, the presentations, or the audience. In this case it came down to the need. Most companies to which we spoke had the resources in-house to handle social media engagement and did not need to outsource the services. They needed to learn how to make their social media efforts more efficient and effective. Therefore, no new business.

The following year I started focusing on corporate crisis planning and training. And as you can guess, the tides turned. I spoke at the same conferences to the same audiences. This time the leads came in more feverishly, and a good portion of the business converted to new clients.

Immediately following the US college admissions scandal in 2019 that implicated a law firm partner, I was contacted by a reporter from the *American Lawyer* to discuss the firm's public handling of the matter. The article "Willkie, College Admissions, and the Crisis Management Playbook" quoted me three times throughout the analysis of the situation. This was yet another outcome of positioning my message around crisis communications.

Lori Loughlin, who served two months in prison after she and her husband pleaded guilty in May 2020 to conspiracy charges for paying $500,000 in bribes to get their daughters into USC, found herself in the news again in October 2021. It was reported that Loughlin "privately" covered the costs of two students' college tuition fees and expenses in the amount of $500,000, as an act of goodwill. This followed her return to acting, which had a separate backlash. Regarding the donation many critics called it a "tactical PR stunt to repair her public image in time for her acting comeback." Based on the available information, I can't help but agree.

As you can see, failing to measure your results could leave you wasting time and money when you create and implement future marketing and public relations plans. Your investment is only of value when you track, measure, and evaluate its effectiveness.

PUBLIC RELATIONS MEASUREMENT LANGUAGE

Whether you engage a professional media measurement company or do it yourself, here is the language of the industry.

AWARENESS (A.K.A. MESSAGE IMPACT): Awareness or message impact measures awareness, attitude, and behavior changes that may have resulted from your public relations efforts. This is usually measured via surveys or focus groups but can be gauged through general feedback received from your PR programs if your budget is limited. Comparative studies are required to determine whether there have been any changes in audience awareness and comprehension levels. This can be accomplished through before-and-after quantitative surveys, tests, control group studies, focus groups, qualitative attitude surveys of target audience groups, and multiple studies that rely on observation, participation, and attitudinal evaluation.

COMPARATIVE AD EQUIVALENCY: The most controversial of all public relations measurement tools, comparative ad equivalency (also known as advertising value equivalency [AVE] and value for placement) measures the financial value of the media coverage you received because of your public relations campaign. It compares what it would have cost to advertise in the same media space, whether it is print, broadcast, or online. The problem is that you are not comparing apples to apples. First, advertising values are always negotiated and are almost never purchased at the one-time rate used for ad equivalency metrics. And the actual value or credibility score of a story in which you are quoted as opposed to an ad you placed is much greater. If you are going to rely on measuring ad equivalency, at the very least, use "audited data," which is the average cost of a media purchase, as opposed to "rate card data."

COMPETITIVE ANALYSIS: Competitive analysis helps you understand where your brand stands in relation to the competition. Review all articles in your target publications to measure the amount of coverage you have garnered in comparison to your competitors during the relevant time prior to your efforts. Contrast current levels of coverage with this measurement to demonstrate the heightened coverage your organization has obtained because of your public relations efforts. The most efficient way to do this is to use a media monitoring tool that provides "share of voice" metrics. Share of voice is explained in more detail below.

EARNED MEDIA: Earned media is unpaid, third-party content that mentions your company, products, services, or individuals typically obtained through media relations.

LEADS GENERATED: Leads generated calculates the number of prospective client leads produced following your public relations campaign. This could be the number of leads that were generated because of a media story or the number generated because of a seminar or any other public relations tool/campaign that the company uses in its communications arsenal.

MEDIA CONTENT ANALYSIS: Media content analysis studies, tracks, and analyzes the content of your public relations messages as they appear in print, television, radio, and online communications. The prime function of media content analysis is to determine whether your key messages, concepts, and themes were disseminated to others via the media. The variables considered in this analysis include the medium, the placement of your message, the mention of the executive's or company's name, the subject of the placement, and the subjective value of the overall piece.

MEDIA COVERAGE: Media coverage measures the number of successful placements, the type of media within which the mentions are located, and the audience who reads, views, or listens to that media.

MEDIA DEMAND: Media demand is determined by whether the media proactively responded to the press materials that you supplied. Did reporters call? Did you land interviews? Did the television cameras roll? Over time did the media reach out to you or your company's executives as a source for quotes?

A notable example of this is when Furia Rubel positioned a lawyer from McGlinchey Stafford in New Orleans as a subject-matter source regarding vaccine mandates. Kelly Mack, the firm's senior business development manager, said, "This is a great example of getting our attorneys out there on a hot topic, how we mobilize and move quickly as a team, the great ROI from this effort, etc. We can include the webinar they are doing next week too. The labor and employment team has hit this hard with a client alert, the media, the webinar. This is great."

MEDIA MAPPING: Media mapping visually demonstrates local, regional, national, or international media placements. Create a map of the United States and use dots or other markers to indicate where placements have appeared. This can visually demonstrate many placements overall (many dots) or a well-controlled regional placement in a localized campaign (clustered dots). The goal is to demonstrate visually that you are reading the correct geotargeted audience.

MEDIA REACH (A.K.A. MEDIA EXPOSURE): Media reach measures the number of people receiving communication via the media, also known as the number of media impressions. To calculate print reach, determine circulation numbers for all publications carrying your messages. This is the raw number of subscribers who were exposed to the story. Multiply print circulation numbers by a "pass-along" factor of 2.5 to determine the number of readers potentially exposed to your story. For some publications, the pass-along rate is much higher; however, it is a publication-by-publication and region-by-region evaluation. Broadcast reach is determined by the number of viewers (rating) at the time of day that your story aired as well as the on-demand viewers after the story originally aired. Number of listeners determines the radio reach. Number of downloads determines the podcast reach. Online reach is determined by the number of unique and repeat visits as measured by tracking software.

MESSAGE PULL-THROUGH: Message pull-through is when your key messages appear in your earned media coverage. For example, if you are consistently promoting your company's community service efforts and an article uses your language or touches on the same key points to describe your company and its efforts, you've achieved message pull-through.

RELATIONSHIP ANALYSIS: Partnerships and joint campaigns are effective public relations approaches. Measuring the value of relationships that are built or strengthened through a campaign is a new challenge. Because the relationships are long-lasting and have the potential for future benefit and collaboration, their value goes beyond traditional publicity measures. Simple measures of immediate relationship value include event attendance, membership figures, newsletter readership, social media engagement, and analysis of each partner's links to other influential companies, organizations, bloggers, and reporters. Relationship analysis is best done using a sophisticated CRM tool.

RETURN ON INVESTMENT (ROI): ROI is traditionally associated with marketing and advertising tactics; however, we are seeing ROI discussions frequently in public relations. ROI is a financial term that determines the incremental gain divided by the cost. Therefore, ROI equals the incremental gain in business divided by the invested resources multiplied by one hundred.

An example of ROI measurement is the value of a new client minus the cost of the initiative to gain that client. Costs include time and expenses, not simply the out-of-pocket expenditures. Let's say that you're an artist and your new line of art was covered in a feature story in a major magazine. If you authored the article, you want to include the value of your time in the analysis. Thereafter, the value of each item sold and attributable to the article goes into the calculation.

SHARE OF VOICE/SHARE OF DISCUSSION: Share of voice (SOV), also known as share of discussion (SOD), is the percentage one company has of the total amount of communication directed to a targeted group. Good SOV is considered a contributing factor to successful awareness campaigns. This captures and compares your company's positive and neutral media coverage to that of your competitors and takes into consideration the media value and tone of the coverage. SOV also subtracts the value of negative stories, which determines the "net favorable media cost of impressions" (NFMCI). The NFMCI is then divided by the total of all competitors to obtain the SOV/SOD percentage score. If this sounds cumbersome, it is. The good news is that there are many measurement services that can help you with these determinations.

SOCIAL MEDIA ENGAGEMENT: Social media engagement represents the number of shares, likes, comments, retweets, re-pins, and other social media interactions that an earned media article receives on the various social networks. In fact, articles with high engagement on social media drive 113% more website traffic than low engaged articles, and they drive 280% more website actions than low engagement articles. Social media engagement is now the biggest driver of consumer behavior.

PUBLIC RELATIONS MEASUREMENT TOOLS

While organizations, such as the Public Relations Society of America (PRSA), offer great measurement resources on their websites (prsa. org), here are several other tools that can help you measure public relations success.

WEBSITE VISITORS AND REFERRALS: Determine how visitors find your website. Visitors can be placed into four categories: owned (from your own website or direct marketing), earned (from content outside your website such as articles or media stories), paid (from advertisements or pay-per-click/PPC), and social (from social media posts). Referrals allow you to see how many new users are coming to your site and how they got there. Google Analytics is a go-to tool to track website visitors and referrals.

SEARCH ENGINE OPTIMIZATION (SEO): Know and use your keywords in your public relations content. This will allow you to measure your position using tools like SEMRUSH to help you follow your position on Google. Get a complete picture of public relations' digital impact—from driving web traffic to influencing search engine ranking. It also is possible to rank your organization's media coverage and determine which articles had the greatest positive impact on your company's search engine ranking. You can then curate the top-performing articles, share them via social media, add links to your website, and share them via your company's direct electronic communications.

TOPIC CLUSTERS: Google has become much more sophisticated and can evaluate the context of the website in which it finds a piece of content. Marketers will benefit from thinking about topic clusters rather than single pages.

Leslie Richards, chief innovation officer at Furia Rubel Communications, said, "For example, if you're a bank, you would start a content strategy by developing a long page (two thousand words or more) that provides a comprehensive overview of the topic 'business banking.' We sometimes refer to this as a 'pillar page.' Once this page is published, you'll create other, related pages and create an internal linking structure with pages related to your pillar page."

Richards said, "You might have a blog post that talks about business lines of credit and another page about money market accounts, a blog about international transactions, and yet another about cash management. You create links that go back and forth between your pillar page and these related pages. You can think of the pillar page as your hub with spokes around it, which are your other pieces of content.

"When Google crawls the landing page of 'business banking,' it follows the links as it catalogs the site content. When developed strategically, this content will help establish your site as an authoritative resource on the topic."

MENTIONS: Mentions are what people are saying about you. To help show the effectiveness of your PR campaigns, keep track of your specific mentions and which campaigns they came through. Try setting up Google Alerts to help track mentions of your name. You can set up multiple alerts for different things you would like to track. You can also pay for numerous services (included below) that track and measure mentions for you.

ENGAGEMENT, LEADS, AND RETENTION: You can track target audience engagement in various ways with your company because of your PR efforts. Engagement comes in many forms. Look at social media likes, comments, and shares; website queries and form completion; direct communications with your organization and its employees; increased media coverage and quotes because of thought leadership; increased new business from existing clients; new retained clients; and ongoing engagements with existing clients.

PUBLIC RELATIONS MEASUREMENT AND MONITORING RESOURCES

Select the suitable options for measuring and monitoring your public relations campaigns. Some services focus on one form of media only, such as radio, television, print, or social media. Others provide more comprehensive services.

Below are resources that are available to help you monitor and measure your public relations campaigns.

- Agility PR
- Bandwidth
- Burrelles
- CARMA International
- Cision | TrendKite
- Converseon
- CoverageBook
- Critical Mention
- Memo
- Mention
- Muck Rack
- Nielsen
- Onclusive
- PublicRelay
- RepTrak
- Signal AI

- Digimind
- Falcon AI
- Google Analytics
- HubSpot
- Meltwater
- Sprinklr
- Sprout Social
- Talkwalker
- Trust Insights
- UNICEPTA

Another tool, which requires more of an explanation, is a client relationship management system (CRM). CRM uses software to track and access information about past, current, and potential clients. A CRM provides a central database of information about people and companies important to the organization, including clients, prospects, referral sources, and other business contacts. The CRM also tracks information related to those contacts, such as activities, notes, financial information, industries, relationships, and touch points with the company. The system can help track business development information, public relations engagement, social media engagement, pitches, requests for proposals, and referrals. Through a CRM system, client interactions can be logged, referenced, and cross-referenced by the organization.

Chris Fritsch, CRM success consultant and founder of CLIENTSFirst Consulting, said, "CRM systems are extremely powerful. Key stakeholders need to determine what they want to accomplish and why. They need to understand how they can use CRM to improve internal and external communications and client service and, ultimately, to affect their bottom line positively."

CRM data helps management understand where the company's business development, marketing, and public relations time is being spent. A CRM also helps keep track of who oversees each lead to avoid a situation in which executives or business development managers contact the same client. Understanding the relationships that a company has with its target audiences, such as current and past clients and referral sources, is only the starting point. A CRM can provide objective data that helps the organization better manage its relationships and investments.

"Assuming the CRM data is maintained and accurate, companies can leverage that data for business development and to understand the sales pipeline and media opportunities," said Jasmine Trillos-Decarie, chief client service officer at Lathrop GPM LLP, a full-service Midwestern Am Law 200 law firm.

Trillos-Decarie added, "A robust CRM system tells us who the executives are talking to, how often they are in communication, and essentially who knows who and how they know them. It allows us to paint a picture and understand the depth of relationships to leverage those relationships for better client service and business development."

Businesses can benefit from platforms that are either installed or cloud based. There is a wide range of options such as Salesforce, HubSpot, Microsoft Dynamics, Apptivo, Pipedrive, Peppermint Technology, and others. The most important thing is to assess your needs and then do your homework. Determine which platform will work best for your company and industry, then dive in.

Alternatively, some companies use back-office platforms that have a CRM component (such as Microsoft Excel or Google Sheets), which can be used, to some extent, to manage and track information and interactions.

Information gained through a CRM system is vital to marketing and public relations because it provides data to validate the continuation of efforts or adjustments to the marketing plan. The information can be measured and tested against program objectives, and ultimately, it can calculate your ROI.

A CRM system is only as good as the data entered. It is up to company leadership to lead by example. Educate all employees on the company's use of CRM and put processes in place to manage the organization's data so investment in a CRM system pays off.

PUBLIC RELATIONS MEASUREMENT EXAMPLES AND NEW BUSINESS CONVERSIONS

With a data-driven tracking and measuring system in place, it is possible to demonstrate real ROI to prove you are getting business from your communications efforts.

To gather that data, it is important to monitor and listen to what your clients are doing and saying. Below are examples of success stories that demonstrate ROI.

BLOG LEADS TO MEDIA COVERAGE AND NEW CLIENTS: As mentioned previously, Bloomberg Law interviewed Lauren Hoye, one of Willig, Williams & Davidson's labor lawyers, because of a Google search that brought up a relevant blog post she had published on the topic. A prospective client then read the Bloomberg Law article, which was relevant to an issue that the prospective client was facing, and contacted Lauren, leading to a new business opportunity.

MEDIA COVERAGE OF A COMMUNITY BANK FOUNDATION HELPED TO GENERATE $500,000 IN DONATIONS, LEADS TO AWARD: In March 2020, as the coronavirus pandemic began gaining a foothold, a community bank in southeast Pennsylvania partnered with its local United Way chapter to create a COVID-19 Recovery Fund. Public relations led to media coverage of the fund, helping it to attract nearly $500,000 in donations over the ensuing ten months. The funds were distributed as grants to United Way's member agencies to help them deliver COVID-19-related services to clients. Ultimately, the fund provided more than eighty grants to more than forty organizations, directly benefitting more than forty thousand county residents, including thirteen thousand children and six thousand seniors. The following year the community bank won a major award for philanthropy from a local business journal publication.

BLOG GENERATES INVITATION AS GUEST PANELIST AT TRIBECA FILM FESTIVAL AND MEDIA COVERAGE: Panitch Schwarze Belisario & Nadel, LLP, an intellectual property law firm, published a blog highlighting actor Hedy Lamarr's role as an inventor who helped lay the groundwork for the technology that powers the wireless devices we use today. Filmmakers contacted the lawyer who authored the blog as part of their research for the 2017 movie *Bombshell: The Hedy Lamarr Story*. After assisting the producers with their research, the lawyer was invited to attend the Tribeca Film Festival and serve as a panelist along with executive producer Susan Sarandon, producer Alexandra Dean, and actor Diane Kruger.

PR GENERATES FULL-HOUSE REGISTRATION FOR BEHAVIORAL HEALTH PROVIDER EVENT: Public relations, including media coverage, event listings, and a social media campaign, helped a behavioral health provider attract record attendance at an event in honor of Suicide Prevention Awareness Month. It was the inaugural event for a newly created nonprofit educational arm of a behavioral health provider and helped the organization establish credibility and trustworthiness in a crowded marketplace. Attendance generated service-related inquiries to the provider; health care privacy laws prevent the provider from sharing personally identifying case information.

MEDIA OUTREACH LANDS *GOOD MORNING AMERICA* SEGMENT ALONGSIDE GLORIA ALLRED: In the story about Stewart Ryan, the lawyer with Philadelphia law firm Laffey, Bucci & Kent and former prosecutor in the Bill Cosby case, Ryan garnered significant media coverage, including an appearance on *Good Morning America* and an interview with the Associated Press. The combined print, broadcast, and online coverage reached an audience of approximately seven hundred million and has since led to new business for the firm.

MEDIA RELATIONS ATTRACTS NEW CLIENTS: Furia Rubel coordinated media relations for a personal injury law firm that handled cases against an international furniture manufacturer. The furniture in question often tipped over and severely injured or killed many toddlers in the United States. There were recalls because of the product defect, and since the filing of the first case, media coverage has ranged from Law.com and Law360.com to *USA Today* and *Good Housekeeping* magazine. As a result of the media coverage, which began years ago and is ongoing, the firm continues to hear from families affected by the manufacturing defect, bringing them on as new clients.

THE CASE FOR PUBLIC RELATIONS MEASUREMENT

Assessing the success or failure of specific public relations programs, strategies, and activities and their impact on improving and enhancing your company's relationships with key audiences is an important discipline.

Understand that ways to measure public relations programs continue to evolve.

Take ownership of your public relations landscape to attract followers. Bring in specialty public relations agencies to help you stay on top of trends and help you evaluate the success of your communication efforts.

CHAPTER 13

PLANNING FOR A CRISIS

"THE CRISIS YOU HAVE TO WORRY ABOUT
MOST IS THE ONE YOU DON'T SEE COMING."

—MIKE MANSFIELD

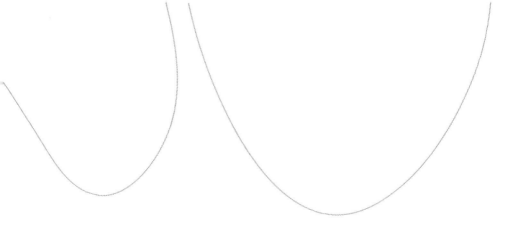

E veryday public relations is about proactive communications—things you can do to retain existing clients and customers and gain new ones. But preparing for and managing a crisis is an essential public relations strategy, as expected and unexpected crises hit companies every day.

Najja R. Orr, Philadelphia Corporation for Aging's president and CEO, said, "The crisis that you don't anticipate is the one to fear the most. At PCA we plan for anything that can impact older adults sixty-plus."

He said, "We know, for example, during the summer months that older adults can be more susceptible to heat emergency, so we continuously plan for that. It takes an entire community and a comprehensive process to mitigate risk and save lives when the temperatures go above one hundred degrees. PCA works as a strategic team to be proactive and communicate critical information so those who are most vulnerable are prepared. Our entire staff is involved, and each member plays a vital role, from our senior centers to our Helpline to our communications staff to our care managers to our collaborative partners and community members. Proper planning, analysis, review, and retuning helps to save lives."

There are many types of crises that can be planned for and anticipated—essentially, it's not if but when a crisis will happen. We see examples every day.

On October 4, 2021, Facebook experienced its worst outage since 2008. Facebook, Instagram, and WhatsApp were offline for more than six hours. During those hours rumors and speculation were global.

The day before, in fact, *60 Minutes* revealed the identity of the whistleblower who leaked private internal research to both the *Wall Street Journal* (*WSJ*) and the United States Congress. The documents, first reported in a series of *WSJ* stories, revealed that the company's executives understood the negative impacts of Instagram among younger users and that Facebook's algorithm enabled the spread of misinformation, among other things.

In that interview Frances Haugen, a former product manager on Facebook's civic misinformation team, accused Facebook of "betraying democracy."

Haugen pointed to the 2020 election as a turning point at Facebook. She said Facebook had announced it was dissolving the Civic Integrity team, to which she was assigned, after the election. A few months later, social media communications would be a key focus in the wake of the January 6 insurrection at the US Capitol.

"When they got rid of Civic Integrity, it was the moment where I was like, 'I don't trust that they're willing to invest what needs to be invested to keep Facebook from being dangerous,'" Haugen told *60 Minutes*.

On the same day as the global outage, Facebook shares dropped by nearly 5 percent.

Facebook eventually took to Twitter to communicate with its platforms' users:

In another statement they said, "To the huge community of people and businesses around the world who depend on us: we're sorry. We've been working hard to restore access to our apps and services and are happy to report they are coming back online now. Thank you for bearing with us."

Weeks later, on October 28, 2021, Facebook's founder Mark Zuckerberg announced that the corporate name had changed to "Meta" to emphasize the company's metaverse vision. I can't help but wonder how much the timing of this rebranding had to do with Haugen blowing the whistle on Facebook. On the same day as Zuckerberg's announcement, a securities class-action lawsuit was filed on behalf of investors who purchased or acquired the securities of Facebook, Inc. (Nasdaq: FB), from November 3, 2016, through October 4, 2021.

In another example one of the top five law firms in the United States, Latham & Watkins, had its chair scandalized when William Voge was accused of sexting a woman he never met in person. Within hours the story was covered on most legal and financial media outlets, including Law360.com, Law.com, Above the Law, the *Wall Street Journal*, the *ABA Journal*, the *Financial Times*, Reuters, Bloomberg Big Law Business, and others. While Voge resigned soon after the accusations were made public, the scandal did not spare the law firm from reputation damage, even though the firm had declared $3 billion in revenues a month before the story broke.

The sad reality is that companies can (and do) plan to manage sexual harassment claims against their employees and executives—it is an all-too-common occurrence. But what about the crisis that leaves you feeling like an athlete who got their clock rung on the field of play?

While I was writing the first edition of this book, the US college admissions scandal implicating Willkie Farr & Gallagher's now former cochairman Gordon Caplan broke in the national media. The *American Lawyer*, which covered the story closely, quoted me:

> "There is no way anyone could have guessed that something like this would happen. It's out of left field, which is exactly why there's such public outrage," said Gina Rubel, a lawyer and marketer who routinely puts together crisis preparation plans for law firms.

I went on to publish "Crisis Lessons in the Immediate Aftermath of the College Admissions Scandal" for an industry trade publication because there was much to learn from how the matter was handled.

Sarah Larson, the executive vice president of Furia Rubel Communications and a former investigative reporter, said, "If recent years have shown us nothing else, it's that the risk to an organization's reputation posed by the possibility of a public crisis has grown exponentially in the digital age. Today we firmly believe that *it's not a matter of if a crisis will happen; it's a matter of when.*"

She said, "Whether the crisis involves the revelation of election-swaying data mining through the world's dominant social media platform (Facebook), a data breach at a leading global hotel chain (Marriott), or viral video of rats scurrying over hamburger buns at a Delaware fast food joint (Burger King), we've seen several examples over the past year of what not to do when your organization is faced with a crisis. Not responding quickly enough, not taking responsibility, and not acknowledging the harm done to customers are among the many don'ts exemplified in these scenarios."

Sarah shares an example of (mostly) successful communications in a high-stakes, high-pressure situation, along with lessons that all organizations can learn from the public outcry over the public arrest of two men who were guilty of nothing more than being in public while Black at a Philadelphia outpost of the world's largest coffeehouse brand, Starbucks.

WAITING WHILE BLACK

Business partners Rashon Nelson and Donte Robinson, both twenty-three, were doing what thousands of people do every day—waiting to meet an acquaintance at a Starbucks for a business meeting over coffee. They had met at that particular Starbucks near Rittenhouse Square several times before, and Robinson had been a customer there since he was fifteen.

But this time, they did not order anything while they were waiting to meet with Philadelphia real estate investor Andrew Yaffe. When one of the men asked to use the restroom, the manager told him the toilets were for paying customers only and reportedly asked him to purchase something or to leave. When the pair did not leave, the manager called the police to remove them. The two men, who are Black, were handcuffed and led out of the store.

The arrests were videotaped by other store patrons, one of whom — Philadelphia-based author Melissa DePino—uploaded it to Twitter with the comment:

> The police were called because these men hadn't ordered anything. They were waiting for a friend to show up, who did as they were taken out in handcuffs for doing nothing. All the other white people are wondering why it's never happened to us when we do the same thing.

The video went viral, spurring nationwide criticism of both the city police department and the coffee chain, as well as protests outside the Starbucks location in Center City, Philadelphia.

STARBUCKS RESPONDS SLOWLY, THEN SWIFTLY

When your brand is in the harsh glare of a media spotlight and is the frenzied focus of an internet mob, it can be hard to think calmly and coolly. That's why we advise all organizations, from global companies to local nonprofits, to draft and regularly update a crisis communications plan—which we generally call an "incident response communications plan" (because the first rule of successfully managing a crisis is, generally, to not call it a crisis).

The response from Starbucks to the arrests in its Philadelphia store on Thursday, April 12, was at first slow and lackluster. The company posted a generic apology to Twitter two days later, on Saturday, April 14, but its general wording may as well have been addressing something as insignificant as an order mix-up.

The short, impersonal statement did nothing to reassure the public that the company was taking the incident seriously. #BoycottStarbucks flooded social media platforms all weekend as outrage grew. Protestors, meanwhile, flooded the Center City Starbucks location to demand that the manager be fired.

The next day, on Sunday, Starbucks CEO Kevin Johnson weighed in personally, with a far more meaningful statement that concluded, "You can and should expect more from us. We will learn from this and be better." He then traveled personally to Philadelphia to meet with city leaders and the two men who had been arrested. Johnson later spoke with the city's largest newspapers, calling the incident "reprehensible" and pledging to "take appropriate action to make sure it doesn't happen again."

The following day, on Monday, April 16, Johnson appeared from Philadelphia on *Good Morning America* to repeat that commitment.

Starbucks started out on the wrong foot in this situation, taking too long to respond. This happens quite often when organizations are still gathering the facts to determine what had actually happened. The response likely was further delayed because of the timing; the men were arrested on Thursday morning, released after midnight (with no charges), and the video spread further on Friday and Saturday. The weekend undoubtedly delayed the company's response time.

In the end Starbucks did many things right.

Here are lessons that other organizations can learn from this incident:

TAKE PERSONAL RESPONSIBILITY: CEOs of global brands are busy people. It would have been easy for Johnson to make some phone calls and continue with his schedule. But he cleared his calendar and traveled to Philadelphia to address the situation in person.

OWN THE MISTAKE: Johnson was clear and unequivocal in condemning the incident and not trying to explain it away or contextualize it: "Calling the police was wrong; it should not have happened."

DISCIPLINE THE EMPLOYEE: When a representative of a company treats a customer poorly, many people want to see a public acknowledgement of wrongdoing. Johnson did lay much of the blame at the manager's feet, saying, "This comes down to an individual incident and an individual leader's decision...This particular incident does not reflect who we are as a company." Within days the manager no longer worked at the Starbucks.

EXAMINE THE POLICIES: When something goes wrong, it is easy to throw one employee under the bus and leave it at that. It is harder to examine the policies and beliefs within a company's culture that allowed the incident to happen. Johnson did not stop with parting ways with the manager. He ordered a full, company-wide review of policies and training, pledging to do the hard work to address systemic beliefs, not just one person's behavior.

IMPLEMENT NEW TRAINING: In the wake of the incident and the subsequent policy review, Johnson ordered all of Starbucks's more than eight thousand US stores to close for a day to undergo mandatory racial-bias education. The session was designed to "address implicit bias, promote conscious inclusion, prevent discrimination, and ensure everyone inside a Starbucks store feels safe and welcome."

REINFORCE COMPANY VALUES: In his communications Johnson said Starbucks wanted to learn from its mistakes and forge a path forward consistent with its core values. "We work to be a different kind of company. A company that believes in using our scale for good. A company that believes that the pursuit of profit is not in conflict with doing social good."

Finally, perhaps the most important lesson:

BE DEMONSTRABLY AUTHENTIC: Johnson communicated directly with the company's target audiences through several channels, including news interviews, in-person meetings, and written statements. But he also filmed an informal, unedited, unpolished (you can even hear someone knocking on a door in the background) personal video message while in Philadelphia so viewers could hear from him directly. That transparency and lack of guile went a long way to restoring trust with Starbucks's primary consumers, who, steeped in a world of fake news, Photoshop, and talking points, crave authenticity from the companies they support.

People make mistakes, and organizations need to be prepared to proactively avoid crises when possible and to effectively respond to them when they do occur. Developing a crisis communications plan is a key step for any organization that wants to be prepared before the white-hot spotlight of a public crisis falls on them.

While the Starbucks matter has died down and the journalists have moved on, scandals, rumors, lawsuits, and many other types of crises will happen every day with companies both big and small.

In life and business, reputation is everything. It only takes one misstep to cause damage to a company and its executives.

IS YOUR ORGANIZATION PREPARED FOR CRISIS?

While not all incidents rise to the level of a crisis, the public relations industry is witnessing an enormous spike in the need for crisis communications and crisis management plans.

There is a reason the growth in chief ethics officers in the C-suite is predicted. With the economic slowdown, preemptive layoffs, disgraced executives, frequent lack of diversity and inclusion in corporate C-suites and boards, data breaches and cyberattacks, the #MeToo movement, citizen journalism, the rise of corporate criminality, war in eastern Europe, and so much more, it is foolish for any business to believe it does not need a crisis management plan.

This is not only an issue for businesses. It is also an issue for your clients. According to a 2018 Crisis Management Benchmarking Report published by Morrison & Foerster and Ethisphere, "*A clear majority of companies do not feel as prepared as they should be to respond to an unexpected crisis event.*"

If that is not enough, recent statistics on cyberattacks indicate that every eleven seconds, a business falls victim to a ransomware attack; 66

percent of small and medium-sized businesses have experienced cyberat-tacks on operational infrastructure, with 76 percent of those companies based in the US; and the global cost of online crime is expected to reach $10.5 trillion annually by 2025, up from $3 trillion in 2015.

No matter the type of business you manage, understanding why you need a crisis management plan, and a crisis management team, is imperative. This chapter discusses the necessity of a crisis management plan and crisis management team and illustrates real-life examples of well-implemented crisis responses.

The time is now to prepare for not what if but when your business is hit with a crisis.

IDENTIFY YOUR CRISIS MANAGEMENT TEAM

Companies, big and small, need to identify their crisis management team.

When identifying your team, use the Crisis Management Team Roster, which can be found in the appendix.

In small companies the team includes owners, outside counsel, and third-party partners. For midsize and big organizations, the team will be more inclusive of internal resources.

Consider the following list as you develop your crisis man-agement team:

- Key executives: chief executive officer (CEO), chief operations of-ficer (COO), chief financial officer (CFO), chief information officer (CIO), executive director
- Spokesperson (this may vary depending on the location, type, and size of the incident)
- Chief marketing officer (CMO) or the equivalent (third-party marketing, website, and social media management support should be on your crisis management team, as they often handle the dissemination of your company's information)
- Head of public and media relations (internal or external or both)
- Information technology (IT) / cybersecurity team (may be internal

or external depending on the size of the company)
- Security (while most businesses do not have a security detail, it is essential to have a relationship with your building's security experts and your local police department if a need for their assistance arises)
- General counsel, outside counsel, insurance counsel (most matters have legal ramifications)

Crisis management team members play a significant role in protecting the organization. Maintain detailed contact information for the crisis management team members (update quarterly) with correct names, titles, cell and home numbers, and email addresses so you may reach them as soon as you learn about an incident.

Identify each member's roles and responsibilities and how those responsibilities differ depending on the scenario. For instance, if your company is dealing with workplace violence, your executive and security officers may take the lead on all issues, whereas your CIO and IT team may take the lead on a cyber breach.

MAINTAIN YOUR COMPANY'S POLICIES

Various policies may come into play during the management of a crisis. Keep all your organization's workplace policies with your crisis management plan. If your company does not maintain workplace policies, now is an excellent time to create them. It is also important to ensure every level of your organization is included within the plan. Crisis policies that are communicated to, and understood by, everyone are more likely to be followed.

The policies that may prove useful when dealing with a crisis include the following:

- Call management
- Cybersecurity policy
- Email/web query management
- Insurance policy
- Media policy
- Notification requirements (i.e., data breach)
- Personnel policy
- Social media policy
- Technology policy
- Security policy
- Surveillance policy
- Work-from-home policy

CRISIS SCENARIOS

In recent years well-known companies have experienced many crises.

HEADLINES:

TikTok Faces Scrutiny in State Attorneys General Probe of Online Harms to Children

Amazon Impersonators Stole $27 Million in a Year

Sexual Misconduct Complaint Filed Against Ex–New York Governor Cuomo

T-Mobile Says Hacker Gained Access to Employee Email Accounts, User Data

Facebook Shutdown Costs over $230 Million in Six Hours

Pinterest Shareholders Sue over "Toxic" Work Culture

Visa and Mastercard to Investigate Financial Ties to Pornhub

Workers' Comp Rates to Jump in Amazon's Washington Fulfillment Centers Due to Hazards

Southwest Warns 6,800 Employees of Impending Layoffs, a First for the Airline

Charter Jet CEO Charged with Sex Trafficking Young Girls

The Death of Zappos's Tony Hsieh: A Spiral of Alcohol, Drugs, and Extreme Behavior

Mechanic Dies Following Workplace Injury at UPS Centennial Ground Hub

Marriott Discloses New Data Breach Impacting 5.2 Million Hotel Guests

Unfortunately, there are hundreds of headlines like these daily.

The types of crisis scenarios businesses face include:
- **CONFRONTATIONAL:** boycott, demonstrations, forced shutdown, protest, public scrutiny, strike, war/conflict
- **FINANCIAL:** acquisition, bankruptcy, devaluation, economic downturn, lost revenue, investor pull-outs, supply chain disruption, uncontrolled debt
- **MALEVOLENCE:** bribery, equipment or product tampering or sabotage, extortion, kidnapping of employee
- **NATURAL:** earthquake, health (pandemic), weather disaster, wildfire
- **ORGANIZATIONAL/LEGAL:** deception, government investigation, high-profile litigation, human rights violation, lawsuit, organizational misconduct, poor judgment/lack of management values

- **PERSONNEL:** criminal wrongdoing, death or departure of key executives, board members, employees or staff, discrimination, employee misconduct, ethical violation, executive disputes, harassment, insider trading, misconduct, employee wellness issues (addiction, depression, suicide)
- **REGULATORY:** OSHA and other safety violations, licensure, overvaluation, sanctions, tax reporting
- **REPUTATIONAL:** negative publicity, rumors, social media attack, scandal, spear campaign, wellness issues
- **TECHNOLOGICAL:** cybersecurity, data breach, failed technologies, ransomware, malware, theft and disclosure of trade secrets
- **WORKPLACE VIOLENCE:** active shooter, employee assault, terrorist, robbery, workplace injuries

CYBERSECURITY, WORKPLACE VIOLENCE, EQUITY, AND BEHAVIORAL HEALTH

CYBERSECURITY

All companies should begin with preparing a cybersecurity response plan and then flesh out other scenarios.

Many corporations are prime targets for hackers and cyberattacks. When successful it is not only the company's information at risk; it also affects employees, past employees, and clients' personal and corporate intelligence.

Remember the Panama Papers? The unprecedented leak of 11.5 million files from the database of the world's fourth-biggest offshore law firm, Mossack Fonseca, was devastating. That was only the beginning. Cyberattacks have become a direct and predictable threat to all companies, big and small.

Cybersecurity is a specialized area and requires advanced knowledge of your company's IT systems, monitoring systems, cyber insurance policies, whether the insurance carrier requires the organization to bank cryptocurrency, how each type of cyberattack works and the technologies you need to protect your company, business continuity planning, and more.

A well-designed crisis management plan is a critical aspect of preparation.

WORKPLACE VIOLENCE

According to the National Safety Council, two million US workers will become victims of violence at work, eighteen thousand workplace assaults are logged weekly, one in four employees is a victim of workplace violence, and every seven seconds, a worker is injured at work.

Like cybersecurity, workplace violence plans require different management tactics from identifying a threat to maintaining a safe environment.

Businesses should have plans to tackle workplace violence and up-to-date crisis management plans, as we are confronted with active shooters and terrorist attacks now more than ever.

Ask: Does the emergency response plan provide an adequate level of employee safety? Is there a shelter-in-place location? Is there an assembly location? How will your company ensure that all employees are safe?

There are key components to designing a crisis management plan for workplace violence. Create a policy that prevents workplace violence, and involve everyone in the line of communication—management, facilities, communications, and security. Conduct mock drills to provide training to your employees to survive an active shooting. Consider providing ALICE training (alert, lockdown, inform, counter, and evacuate). Free ALICE training and resources are available at www.AliceTraining.com. Identify a potentially volatile employee to prevent an attack. Have a crisis plan specific to workplace violence.

While workplace violence is extremely difficult to predict, there are warning signs, which include:

- Excessive use of alcohol or drugs

- Unexplained absenteeism, change in behavior, or decline in job performance
- Depression, withdrawal, or suicidal comments
- Resistance to changes at work or persistent complaining about unfair treatment
- Violation of company policies
- Emotional responses to criticism, mood swings
- Paranoia

When workplace violence takes place, follow safety protocol above all else. Deal with the safety of people first—all else can wait. Communicate immediately with first responders.

Maintain a list that includes the contact information for essential first responders and utility and support services, such as electrical power, water, sewer, gas, emergency, telecommunications, and transportation. Include this list with your crisis management team list. Maintain an up-to-date media list.

Conduct safety training. Ensure communication capability that includes satellite phones strategically placed within the building, a website with designated areas for posting messages, group text messaging, a toll-free call-in number, private social media channels, and mass email capabilities where individuals can relay messages.

Use free resources to train your employees on how to handle workplace violence. For example, the FBI has training videos, posters, and other resources available for active shooter response on its website at fbi.gov/about/partnerships/office-of-partner-engagement/active-shooter-resources.

DIVERSITY, EQUITY, AND INCLUSION (DE&I)

Corporate marketing and business development teams often serve as the gatekeepers for compelling communication channels that influence target audiences.

To ensure your company takes important steps regarding antiracism, antiageism, antisexism, and other illegal workplace biases, assess your corporate DE&I data and efforts.

Communicate the measurable steps both internally and externally, and identify the ways your company will refine its plans. Speak to your clients openly and often. Ask them what they want and expect regarding DE&I initiatives.

Prioritize accountability and transparency, which are critical to moving toward achieving equality for all and ending social injustice. Advocate for systemic change. Be proactive. Speak up. If you are not a member of a diverse community, educate yourself before you speak, ensuring you understand the issues and know how to effectively ask sensitive questions.

Build DE&I efforts into your community engagement efforts. Be prepared to answer questions from the media about your organization's DE&I statistics and how furloughs and layoffs may impact your company's numbers. Take seriously any allegations of corporate policy violations regarding DE&I efforts, and remedy as appropriate.

"We've got to be more competitive to be viable, looking toward what we want the world to be and what the market conditions will dictate, not to where the world is now," said David Brown, diversity adviser to the office of the dean of Temple University's Klein College of Media and Communication.

Today we find ourselves in much more of a global environment. The people that we are attracting are looking for a more diverse, equitable, and inclusive environment in which they work. And if they don't find it, they'll invest in it to make it better, or they'll leave and then invest in it to make wherever they land better. It becomes something that we must do for the right reasons, and the reasons have always been right, but we now have the wherewithal and the resources to make it happen.

On Record PR Podcast: The Importance of Diversity in Education, Public Relations, and Corporations, with David Brown of Temple University

BEHAVIORAL HEALTH

Does your crisis management plan consider behavioral health issues? If not, it should.

Many white-collar professions struggle with problematic alcohol dependency and are more susceptible to mental health issues like drug abuse, depression, stress, panic, anxiety, social alienation, isolation, and even suicide compared to general population.

"Addiction is not insane. It's a biological, brain-based process," said Brian Cuban, author of *The Addicted Lawyer*. "It affects so many of us—lawyers, our loved ones, ourselves, our siblings, our children, our friends—and if we look at the statistics, it's brutal. In 2020, if we want to talk about only opioids, there were over ninety thousand fatal opioid overdoses in 2020. That's just opioids. We have a problem."

On Record PR Podcast: Author Brian Cuban Talks about The Addicted Lawyer *and the Addiction Crisis among Lawyers*

As mentioned throughout this book, it is not a matter of whether a crisis will happen; it is a matter of when. We need to talk about behavioral health issues now. Employees are corporations' most valuable assets.

Crisis management plans should include preemptive measures to take care of their company's assets and avoid losing their company's assets, potential malpractice claims, and ethics violations. How can you adequately introduce well-being for employees? Identify individuals who may be reluctant to seek help. Introduce behavioral health support and wellness initiatives through the company's human resources department. Create strategies to handle behavioral health issues and tactics to maintain confidentiality within the organization. Create a judgment-free zone. Mental health stigma is an issue. Design assistance programs to encourage employees to speak openly about what they are going through.

DETERMINE THE TARGET AUDIENCE TO INFLUENCE IN A CRISIS

Once you have identified the various scenarios, ask whom you want or need to influence depending on each scenario.

Internal and external audiences, such as employees (and sometimes their families), clients, customers, referral sources, media, third-party partners, stakeholders, and the community at large, may need to be informed regarding the crisis.

Response time to a crisis should be as soon as safely and reasonably possible.

Always include your company's general counsel, and if you do not have in-house counsel, involve your outside counsel early on. Better safe than sorry. Think about evidence preservation.

If you have an external public relations team that assists with crisis response, determine what information the team may and may not be privy to and when. This is crucial, especially if certain information is or may become privileged. The crisis management team must be cautious to avoid transferring confidential information.

MONITOR, TRACK, AND REFINE THE CRISIS PLAN

Throughout the crisis and as it plays out, monitor all forms of communication. This means collecting information from your organization's employees regarding questions they received from clients, customers, prospects, media, and others regarding the incident. Monitor the media. Know what is being said on social media. Keep copious notes.

Once life has seemingly returned to normal, or seminormal, conduct a postmortem review of how the crisis unfolded, how it was handled, and what might be done differently.

Evaluate the effectiveness of the crisis management team. Evaluate the effectiveness of your response tactics. Update your crisis scenarios and response tactics in the crisis management plan. Update your contact lists (crisis management team, media lists, first responders' lists). Then retrain the crisis management team.

As Sarah Larson said, "Whether the crisis involves the revelation of election-swaying data mining through the world's dominant social media platform (Facebook), a data breach at a leading global corporation, or the death of a CEO, refine your crisis plan, and monitor your organization's reputation after the crisis has passed."

EXAMINE THE POLICIES: When something goes wrong, it is easy to throw one employee under the bus and leave it at that. It is harder to examine the policies and beliefs within a company's culture and how they could have allowed the incident to happen. Do not stop when the crisis is over. Order a company-wide review of policies and training, pledging to do the hard work to address and rectify weaknesses.

And prepare, prepare, prepare. Conduct a mock crisis drill at least once a year so that the employees and crisis management team members get familiar with the crisis management plan and can act confidently when a real crisis takes place.

When you conduct a fire drill, you can evaluate the response of the crisis management team and identify mistakes. Did the building have enough emergency exits? Did the employees remember the location of the fire extinguisher? Was the command post appropriate? Did your crisis plan address off-site backups of your computer data?

A mock crisis drill will help your employees remember how your crisis management plan is designed and should be performed by companies of all sizes, like a fire drill.

Crises happen, and organizations must prepare to manage them proactively and respond effectively.

CRISIS MANAGEMENT TIPS TO LIVE BY

Remember, there is a difference between reacting and responding to a crisis. The best way to respond is to have a plan.

You are always "on," even at a private reception.

The best defense against a crisis is a good offense. Create a crisis management plan, no matter the size of your organization.

Crisis plans need to consider all audiences—staff, clients, customers, media, and referral sources.

Some vulnerabilities need to be addressed by all companies; look at the warning signs, and plan for the crisis before one hits.

Always have a few big evergreen stories in your pocket to balance bad news.

Never say "no comment" to the media.

Make sure you have the correct facts before going on the record. If you must prioritize speed versus effectiveness, choose the latter. Make sure you are accurate.

If there are public inaccuracies, correct them.

Have your messages (boilerplate and evergreen) ready to prepare for a crisis.

Even if you do not have a crisis communications plan, act today by identifying who is in charge when a crisis hits.

If you think your business does not need a crisis plan, think again.

AFTERWORD

A NOTE ABOUT GOING VIRAL

"To go viral you need to be nimble, you need to know your market, and you need to be creative. You need to be able to try things that no one's tried before."

—**STEFANIE TRILLING**

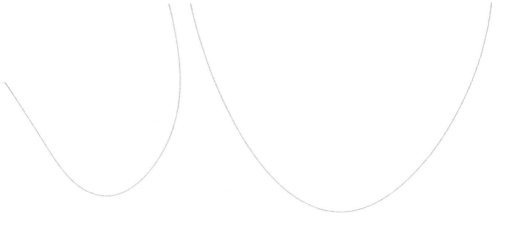

G oing viral amid a global pandemic: this was the last thing on my mind when I began painting parodies of children's book covers in the earliest days of New York's stay-at-home orders. The only thing on my mind was figuring out how my family would survive sequestered within our two-bedroom Manhattan apartment for (what I thought at the time would be) two weeks.

Our living room windows overlooked a thruway to some of the largest hospitals in Manhattan, from which a constant stream of sirens served as an unabating reminder that our neighbors and community suffered. Fear and uncertainty gripped all of us, including my then five-year-old and two-year-old. To soothe their anxiety, I brought out the highest-value activities I could, involving the messiest crafts we could find.

One day my kids were painting at the dining room table, and I decided to join in.

I didn't know what to paint, so I looked around and saw a book that we had read earlier in the day: Mo Willems's *An Elephant & Piggie Biggie*. I started painting the characters, and then my mind drifted to something I was worried about relating to COVID-19. I started doodling some cartoon-like coronaviruses into my painting. My daughter looked over and asked, "Do Elephant and Piggie have COVID-19?" It paved the way for a discussion about a hard topic.

My immediate family loved the painting, so I posted it on social media. My friends thought it was hilarious and requested another parody, so I did another book: *Pete the Cat and the Bad Corona*. I posted it, and

I got a great response. I kept doing it and made my posts public when my friends wanted to share them with their friends. From there people I didn't know were messaging me suggestions for book covers to do and telling me how much they liked my work.

I made a social media account specifically for my project because it became too much to manage on my personal page. I continued to post every single day. One night I seemed to be getting a lot of traction, topping at about nine hundred followers in mid-April 2020. The next morning, I woke up, and the number had skyrocketed to more than twenty thousand overnight.

This was completely organic. I didn't do any paid advertising. I didn't pay anyone to manage my campaign. My posts' popularity was purely based on the novelty of what I was doing, catching it at exactly the right moment in the market and not being afraid to try something I had never tried before. I had never painted before in any capacity like this, and I have no formal art training. I figured, "What's the worst thing that's going to happen?"

After the initial panic abated, the wonderful support continued. I receive delightful messages from my fans and have garnered exciting media attention. The story ran on *Good Morning America*, CNN, *PBS NewsHour*, and local Manhattan TV stations and in *Parents* magazine, the *New York Post*, and hundreds of news outlets nationwide.

I could not have planned for such overwhelming attention if I had tried.

Every business wants to create the perfect viral campaign, but that's not how it works. Viral content is organic, and it's about taking a chance to find a spark of creativity that has yet to be uncovered. And it's all about timing.

My advice to those who want to find that spark: be unprepared, because that's when these kinds of things happen. Viral content hits a note that nothing else is hitting at that time in a particular area, whether it is an industry, a geography, or a cultural phenomenon. In the age of COVID-19, the universal sense of uncertainty and fear, combined with the comfort and familiarity many people draw from our collective history with children's books, created the perfect storm.

My paintings drew on a unique collective experience, and they resonated in a way that most commercial campaigns can't. I painted on the fly, with no commercial motives and with no plans for where it would take me. Most corporate campaigns undergo careful curation, created by committee. To go viral you need to be nimble, you need to know your market, and you need to be creative. You must try things that no one's tried before.

The global pandemic has changed all of us. My silver lining has been the opportunity to recenter with my family, allowing me to break down the truest essence of what is important. In a post pandemic society, and I hope we get there one day soon, everyone's story is forever changed, and everyone has an opportunity to rewrite their next chapter, both personally and professionally.

ABOUT THE AUTHOR

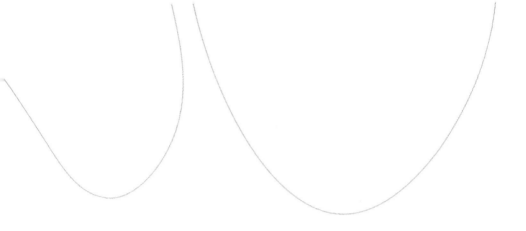

G INA F. RUBEL, ESQ., is the founder and CEO of Furia Rubel Communications, Inc. (www.FuriaRubel.com), an integrated marketing, public relations, crisis communications, and content marketing agency. For more than twenty years, corporate and law firm leaders have called on Gina for strategic corporate communications planning, high-stakes public relations, crisis planning, and incident response support.

A renowned PR expert, author, podcast host, and former practicing attorney, Gina works with clients throughout North America, in Caribbean countries, and in other English-speaking nations. Throughout her career she has advised notable clients including global pharmaceutical companies, international religious organizations, biotechnology companies, banks, government entities and municipalities, nonprofit associations, consumer products and services companies, membership associations, international and national law firms, educational institutions, accounting firms, and technology and manufacturing corporations.

A sought-after speaker, Gina teaches audiences nationwide how to implement ethical, integrated, and measurable communication strategies that help their organizations to meet their business objectives through client and talent retention and acquisition.

Known in the legal industry as a leading expert on legal marketing, public relations, and reputation management, Gina is a Fellow of the College of Law Practice Management and the American Bar Foundation. She also is recognized by Lawdragon as a Global 100 Leading Consultant and Strategist to the legal profession. Gina formed and cochairs the

Philadelphia Bar Association's Law Firm Risk Management Committee—the first of its kind for a bar association—and believes it is every lawyer's duty to understand how various risks can affect their law firms and their clients.

In 2022, Gina was honored by *PRNews* magazine with a Top Women Award in the category of innovation. She and her company received the Business Achievement Award from the Central Bucks Chamber of Commerce. And Gina has been named a Woman of Distinction by the *Legal Intelligencer* and *Philadelphia Business Journal*.

She has been included among Pennsylvania's Best 50 Women in Business and is a *SmartCEO* magazine Brava Award winner. She often is quoted in Law360 and the *American Lawyer* and has appeared on various news programs as a communications expert.

A graduate of Drexel University and Widener University, Delaware Law School, Gina lives in Pennsylvania with her husband, two children, rabbits, chickens, and dogs.

You can follow her on Twitter at @ginarubel, connect on LinkedIn via ginafuriarubel, or email her at gina@furiarubel.com. For more information, go to www.FuriaRubel.com.

APPENDIX

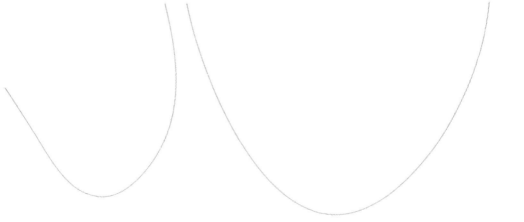

DEVELOPING A PUBLIC RELATIONS PLAN

DEFINE ORGANIZATIONAL BUSINESS GOALS

What are your quantifiable core business goals?

DEFINE YOUR ORGANIZATION'S PUBLIC RELATIONS OBJECTIVES

What do you want to achieve by conducting public relations?

DEFINE HOW YOU WANT TO BE PERCEIVED
How do you want people to perceive you as a corporate executive?

IDENTIFY YOUR TARGET AUDIENCE
Whom do you want to influence?

ESTABLISH YOUR KEY MESSAGES
What do you want and need to say?

CRAFT YOUR CALL TO ACTION

What do you want your audience to think or do because of your message?

PERSUADE YOUR TARGET AUDIENCE TO ACT

Which tactics will reach your audience to accomplish the PR objectives?

MEASURE PUBLIC RELATIONS OUTCOMES

Which KPI will you measure to identify tactical success?

CRAFTING YOUR BRIEF INTRODUCTION

Also known as an elevator speech, a brief introduction is a clear, concise statement about who you are and how you can benefit your target audience. This short statement should support how you want people to perceive you: your reputation.

WHO ARE YOU?

State your name, title, and company affiliation.

WHAT DO YOU DO?

In a sentence state what your job or profession entails.

HOW DOES YOUR WORK BENEFIT OTHERS?

What differentiates you among a pool of others with the same title?

INTERVIEW PREP SHEET

REPORTER'S NAME

MEDIA OUTLET

NOTES FROM RECENT RELATED COVERAGE

KEY ANCHORING MESSAGES

1.

2.

3.

BRIDGING TECHNIQUES/PHRASES TO REMEMBER

BULLET POINTS FOR ADDRESSING THE QUESTIONS YOU MOST DREAD

EVENT EVALUATION SPREADSHEET

Event Name	Date	Name of Organization	# of Anticipated Attendees	Target Audience	Industry

Cost to Attend	Cost to Speak	Cost to Exhibit	Cost to Sponsor	Sponsorship Perks	Previous Company Participation	Anticipated ROI

CRISIS MANAGEMENT TEAM ROSTER

Name	Role	Mobile Phone	Home Phone	Email
KEY EXECUTIVES				
	Chief Executive Officer			
	Chief Operations Officer			
	Chief Financial Officer			
	Chief Information Officer			
	Executive Director			
SPOKESPEOPLE				
	Chief Marketing Officer			
	Head of Public Relations			
INFORMATION TECHNOLOGY				
	Chief Technology Officer			
	Head of Cybersecurity			

SECURITY
Head of Building Security
Fire Warden
Police Precinct

LEGAL
Chief Legal Officer
General Counsel
Outside Counsel
Insurance Counsel